Experiencing the Depths of Jesus Christ:
A Deeper Understanding of the Godhead

By

Prophetess Mary J. Ogenaarekhua

Endorsement

"Experiencing the Depths of Jesus Christ by Prophetess Mary O. is a testimony that the Lord Jesus Himself wants us to know Him and to experience Him in a greater measure. The Lord said in **Amos 3:7** that He reveals His secrets unto His servants the prophets. Therefore, you will find glorious secrets about the Lord Jesus as He reveals Himself to you in your awesome journey through the chapters of this book. I encourage you to read this book because, 'It is the glory of God to conceal a thing: but the honour of kings is to search out a matter -**Proverbs 25:2**.'"

–Lynne Garbinsky, Chief Operations Officer, THGP/MJM, Atlanta, Georgia.

Dedication

I dedicate this book to my Lord Jesus Christ. Lord, You gave me the words to write in this book and I thank You for it because without Your teachings, I will not have anything to write. I also thank You for giving me the grace to write what You taught me. You have done through me concerning this book as it is written in **Psalm 68:11**:

> *"The Lord gave the word: great was the company of those that published it."*

Thanks Lord for teaching me about You; about Your Father and about the Holy Spirit. It is a great honor to have You as my Lord and my Teacher. May this book bring You, the Father and the Holy Spirit much glory.

I also dedicate this book to all those who seek to know the Lord Jesus on a deeper level. May the Lord use it to reveal Himself to you in greater depths as you read it.

Experiencing the Depths Jesus Christ:
A Deeper Understanding of the Godhead

Unless otherwise indicated, all scriptures are quoted from the King James and the New International Versions of the Bible.

Published by: **To His Glory Publishing Company, Inc.**
463 Dogwood Drive, NW
Lilburn, GA 30047
(770) 458-7947
www.tohisglorypublishing.com

This Book is available at:
Amazon.com, BarnesandNoble.com, Booksamillion.com, UK, EU, Canada, Australia, etc.

Also, see the Order Form at the back of this book or call/ email below to order this book.

(770) 458-7947
www.tohisglorypublishing.com
Email: tohisglorypublishing@yahoo.com

ISBN: 978-0-9821900-8-1   or   0-9821900-8-5

Table of Contents

Preface

This book is the second in a series of three books titled; *Experiencing the Depths of God the Father, Experiencing the Depths of Jesus Christ, and Experiencing the Depths of the Holy Spirit.* I wrote them to help people gain a deeper knowledge of the Godhead; also known as the Trinity.

My belief is that if you are totally devoted or sold out to follow the Lord, then you owe it to yourself to know Him in depth and to understand the mysteries that are coded in His Word to help you understand Him in your Christian walk. Therefore, it is my desire that after you have read this book, you will know the Lord Jesus in a much deeper and intimate way than most people can ever dream of.

The Lord told us in **John 8:12** that He is the light of the world and that whoever follows Him will not walk in darkness:

> "Then spake Jesus again unto them, saying, **I am the light of the world: he that followeth me shall not walk in darkness, but shall have the light of life.**"

Therefore, you should purpose in your heart to get to know Him deeper so that He can shine His light on your path as you go through the journey of life. I believe that this book will help you by revealing to you aspects of the Lord Jesus that He reserves for those who are truly serious about getting to know Him intimately. May He bless you as you read it.

—**Dr. Mary J. Ogenaarekhua**

Acknowledgements

Thank You Lord Jesus for calling me to rise up to write what You taught me about the Godhead and what You desire for Your people to know about You and the Godhead in these last days.

I thank you Lynne Garbinsky for your encouragement, dedication and the countless hours that you spent in co-editing and formatting the layout of this book. You are a great friend and a true sister in the Lord. God bless you.

I also thank my students and my fellow Christians that hunger for a deeper understanding of the Lord and the Godhead. Your deep hunger created the opportunity that the Lord used to stir me up to arise and put in a written form for you, what He has taught me. Thank you all for your intense hunger for a greater knowledge of the Father, the Lord, and the Holy Spirit. May He bless you all and all those who will read this book with a deep revelation of Himself.

Chapter 1
Jesus the Young Itinerant Preacher

God's Requirement for the Priesthood

The Lord Jesus showed up on both the scenes of Galilee and Jerusalem as a young itinerant preacher with the ability to work miracles, signs and wonders but the religious leaders refused to acknowledge that He was sent by God. They refused Him because the normal qualification for ministering in those days was to be officially consecrated as a priest by the religious leaders themselves or to be the son of a priest. As a result, the High Priest as well as the other priests, prophets, scribes and rabbis were people that had the "appropriate pedigree" in the priesthood or the Jewish religious system.

This requirement for a "Levitical and later Rabbinical pedigree" by the Jewish leaders was in line with God's stated requirement for the priesthood. It began the day that He gave the priesthood to the tribe of Levi; beginning with Moses, Aaron, and Aaron's sons. As stated in **Exodus 28:1-3**, He gave to Aaron and his sons the position of High Priest and priests:

> "**And take thou unto thee Aaron thy brother, and his sons with him, from among the children of Israel, that he may minister unto me in the priest's office, even Aaron, Nadab and Abihu, Eleazar and Ithamar, Aaron's sons.** 2 And thou shalt make holy garments for Aaron thy brother for glory and for beauty. 3 And thou shalt speak unto all that are wise hearted, whom I have filled with the spirit of wisdom, that they may make Aaron's garments to consecrate him, **that he may minister unto me in the priest's office.**"

God emphasized His requirement for the priesthood in **Malachi 2:4-7**:

"And ye shall know that I have sent this commandment unto you, **that my covenant might be with <u>Levi</u>, saith the LORD of hosts. 5 My covenant was with him of life and peace; and I gave them to him for the fear wherewith he feared me, and was afraid before my name. 6 The law of truth was in his mouth, and iniquity was not found in his lips: he walked with me in peace and equity, and did turn many away from iniquity**. 7 For the priest's lips should keep knowledge, and they should seek the law at his mouth..."

As a result, a person was not considered a legitimate prophet, rabbi or scribe if the person did not have the "appropriate pedigree." For example, John the Baptist's father was a priest, so it was easy for the Jewish leaders to accept him as a legitimate Priest or Prophet. As for the Lord Jesus, He did not have what they considered "the appropriate pedigree."

The Levites Lost the Priesthood

The Levites lost the right to the priesthood succession in the days of the last High Priest called **Eli** and Israel began to have Judges and finally kings. It was the kings that then began to consecrate the various high priests and the kings' established "order of succession" remained in place until the Roman Empire. Therefore, the problem the Jewish leaders had with the Lord was that to them, He came from nowhere and yet, miracles, signs and wonders followed Him everywhere He went. Also, the people recognized that God was with Him but the Pharisees did not know what to do with Him because no priest and no prophet had ever come out of Galilee.

Jesus Spoke Differently

Another thing about the Lord Jesus was that He spoke differently; very differently from all the other rabbis or prophets. In short, He said things that they had never heard before; things that no rabbi or prophet has ever had the audacity to say. For instance, one day, while He was talking to the people; some of whom were already struggling with the fact that He was a Rabbi from Galilee, He said that God was His Father in **John 6:36-44:**

"But I said unto you, <u>That ye also have seen me, and believe not.</u> 37 <u>All that the Father giveth me shall come to me; and him that cometh to me I will in no wise cast out.</u> 38 **For I came down from heaven, not to do mine own will, but the will of him that sent me.** 39 **And this is the Father's will which hath sent me,** that of all which he hath given me I should lose nothing, but should raise it up again at the last day. 40 And this is the will of him that sent me, that every one which seeth the Son, and believeth on him, may have everlasting life**: and I will raise him up at the last day.

41 <u>The Jews then murmured at him, because he said, I am the bread which came down from heaven.</u> 42 **And they said, <u>Is not this Jesus, the son of Joseph, whose father and mother we know</u>? how is it then that he saith, I came down from heaven**? 43 Jesus therefore answered and said unto them, Murmur not among yourselves. 44 **No man can come to me, except the Father which hath sent me draw him**: and I will raise him up at the last day."

God's Promise of a New Covenant and Jesus

Naturally, The Lord Jesus drew the attention of many people; some of whom genuinely needed miracles, while others came to hear His words that they considered unusual.

In other words, some people came to hear Him because they believed in Him while some came to hear Him out of curiosity and yet, others came to Him because they could not believe that the miracles were of God. So, there were many agenda in the hearts of the many people who gathered around Him in those days.

What a lot of the people did not know was that God the Father actually sent the Lord Jesus as His Son to the Jews **to establish a New Covenant**. The covenant that He promised them in **Jeremiah 31:31-34:**

> "Behold, the days come, saith the LORD, that I will make <u>a new covenant</u> with the house <u>of Israel, and with the house of Judah:</u> 32 <u>Not according to</u> **the covenant** <u>that I made with their fathers in the day that I took them by the hand to bring them out of the land of Egypt</u> *(the Old Testament or Covenant);* **which my covenant they brake,** although I was an husband unto them, saith the LORD:
>
> 33 **But this shall be the covenant that I will make with the house of Israel; After those days, saith the LORD, I will put my law in their inward parts, and write it in their hearts; and will be their God, and they shall be my people.** 34 And they shall teach no more every man his neighbour, and every man his brother, saying, Know the LORD: for they shall all know me, from the least of them unto the greatest of them, saith the LORD..."

The children of Israel in their different generations could not keep the terms of the **Old Testament** or the **LAW** that God gave them when they came out of Egypt. As a result of their constant violation of the terms of the commandments or the **LAW**, God sent His Son to fulfill the righteous requirements of the **LAW** and to establish a **New Covenant** — **Hebrews 7:11-19:**

"If therefore perfection were by the Levitical priesthood, (for under it the people received the law,) what further need was there that another priest should rise after the order of Melchisedec, and not be called after the order of Aaron? 12 **For the priesthood being changed, there is made of necessity a change also of the law.**

13 **For he of whom these things are spoken pertaineth to another tribe, of which no man gave attendance at the altar.** 14 **For it is evident that our Lord sprang out of Juda; of which tribe Moses spake nothing concerning priesthood.** 15 And it is yet far more evident: for that after the similitude of Melchisedec there ariseth another priest,

16 **Who is made, not after the law of a carnal commandment, but after the power of an endless life.** 17 For he testifieth, Thou art a priest for ever after the order of Melchisedec. 18 **For there is verily a disannulling of the commandment going before for the weakness and unprofitableness thereof.** 19 For the law made nothing perfect, but the bringing in of a better hope did; by the which we draw nigh unto God."

Furthermore, we are told that **GRACE** and **TRUTH** came by the Lord Jesus Christ. **The Lord Jesus was therefore trying to get the people to make a transition from the LAW** of commandments to the **GRACE** and **TRUTH** that He brought with Him for them:

> "For the law was given by Moses, **but grace and truth came by Jesus Christ**" (John 1:17).

What this means is that the Lord Jesus is the embodiment of **GRACE** and **TRUTH** for everyone that believes in Him. The people no longer have to keep the law of commandments in order to become righteous. Now, faith in Christ brings the GRACE of God which is salvation. This GRACE can only come when one receives the TRUTH which is the Word of God or the Gospel. **God's Word is the truth that does not change** as shown in the scriptures below:

> **"Sanctify them through thy truth: thy word is truth"** (John 17:17).

> **"For ever, O LORD, thy word is settled in heaven"** (Psalm 119:89).

Chapter 2
Jesus as the I AM

Although He drew the attention of all those who heard Him in both Galilee and Jerusalem, what the people did not realize was that the **I AM THAT I AM** was actually the one in their midst in the person of Jesus Christ. As the **I AM**, Jesus had the ability to make the impossible to become possible and He spoke as God and He acted as God. For example, one day, He said to them in **John 8:51-57** that **whoever believes in Him shall never see death!**

Now, you can just imagine the shock in the faces of His audience because all the Jews knew that only God can keep a person from dying; so His words actually caused an uproar:

"Verily, verily, I say unto you, If **a man keep my saying, he shall never see death**. Then said the Jews unto him, <u>Now we know that thou hast a devil. Abraham is dead, and the prophets; and thou sayest, If a man keep my saying, he shall never taste of death</u>. 53 **Art thou greater than our father Abraham, which is dead? and the prophets are dead: whom makest thou thyself?** *(This is the core of the question; who is Jesus?).*

54 Jesus answered, If I honour myself, my honour is nothing: it is my Father that honoureth me; of whom ye say, that he is your God: 55 Yet ye have not known him; but I know him: and if I should say, I know him not, I shall be a liar like unto you: but I know him, and keep his saying.

56 **Your father Abraham rejoiced to see my day: and he saw it, and was glad**. 57 Then said the Jews unto him, Thou art not yet fifty years old, and hast thou seen Abraham...?"

This drew the wrath of not just the leaders but many of those who were listening to Him; including many of His disciples. To them, He really made matters worse by overstepping the boundary between man and God! He was not only saying that if they keep His saying they will never see death, **He was also saying that Abraham who lived hundreds of years before Him saw His days and rejoiced**. These sayings presented a lot of problems to the Jews because He was less than 40 years old. They could not understand how Abraham could have seen His days? They just concluded that He was mad or insane.

So, it is clear that the Lord was totally different from any other rabbi that they had ever seen. To make matters even more perplexing, He says to them in **John 8:58-59:**

> "Verily, verily, I say unto you, **Before Abraham was, I am** (*meaning that He is eternal*). Then took they up stones to cast at him: but Jesus hid himself, and went out of the temple, going through the midst of them, and so passed by."

A lot of the Jews who heard Him wanted to stone Him because they all knew that God's name is **I AM.** It is the name by which God introduced Himself to Moses at the burning bush in **Exodus 3:14**. Therefore, from the perspective of a lot of those listening to Him, it did not make sense for this young Rabbi to come on the scene and make what seems to them as the most outrageous and outlandish statements that anyone could ever make. Nevertheless, many people outside of the Jewish leadership believed Him to be "the Prophet or the Christ." As for the leaders as well as many others, they did not know who He really was as evidenced in **John 7:41-53:**

> "Many of the people therefore, when they heard this saying, said, Of a truth this is the Prophet. 41 Others said, This is the Christ. **But some said, Shall Christ come out of Galilee? 42 Hath**

24

not the scripture said, That Christ cometh of the seed of David, and out of the town of Bethlehem, where David was?

43 So there was a division among the people because of him. 44 **And some of them would have taken him; but no man laid hands on him.** 45 Then came the officers to the chief priests and Pharisees; and they said unto them, Why have ye not brought him?

46 The officers answered, Never man spake like this man. 47 **Then answered them the Pharisees, Are ye also deceived? 48 Have any of the rulers or of the Pharisees believed on him?** 49 But this people who knoweth not the law are cursed. 50 Nicodemus saith unto them, (he that came to Jesus by night, being one of them,)

51 Doth our law judge any man, before it hear him, and know what he doeth? 52 **They answered and said unto him, Art thou also of Galilee? Search, and look: for out of Galilee ariseth no prophet.** 53 And every man went unto his own house."

As you can see, the Jewish leaders in the days of the Lord Jesus did not know that they were dealing with someone whose roots or pedigree went deeper than Galilee. All they knew was that He was Jesus of Nazareth, in the region of Galilee. Galilee was a place where the Greeks, the Samarians and the Jews that were not living by the strict Jewish laws and customs dwelt. As a result, to the Jewish leaders and to the very religious Jews, Galilee was a city where different ethnic groups intermingle and marry. Therefore, they regarded Galilee as a polluted city where interracial people dwelt and where idolatry was practiced.

That is why when Jesus met the woman at the well in John Chapter 4, the woman was shocked that Jesus being a Jew would talk to her when Jesus said to her "give me (water) to drink." To summarize their conversation, she said I am a Samaritan woman and you are a Jew. We cannot have any dealings because the Jews do not deal with Samaritans. Again, the reason for this is because the Jews viewed the Samaritans as unclean due to their way of life. Not only were they not totally sanctified unto God, but they also had a history of mixing with the Romans, the Greeks and other different ethnic groups. This is the reason why Galilee is called **Galilee of nations**.

Therefore, for the Lord Jesus to make the type of claims that He was making was absurd to the Jews. They did not find it amusing that He was making Himself out to be the Son of God. **Actually, they accused Him of blasphemy by making Himself equal to God as the Son of God.** It is unfortunate that even today there are a lot of people in Christendom that if you ask them who Jesus really is, they too will not be able to answer the question.

For instance, if someone from another religion should come to them and ask, "Who is this Jesus that you guys worship?" They cannot <u>fully</u> answer the question because they have not taken the time to find out about who Jesus really is. As a Christian, you have to be able to give such people both an historical account as well as revelation from scriptures about who Jesus really is.

Is Jesus Really the I AM?

To answer this question, we need to look at the "eternal existence" of the Lord Jesus in the next chapter. It is a revelation of the Lord Jesus' existence before He came into the earth as the manifested Son of God.

I AM means: Ever existing, eternal and able to be or do anything that He wants.

Chapter 3
Jesus' Eternal Existence

Jesus as Wisdom

Before He came into the world as God's SON, the Lord Jesus had always existed in eternity as **WISDOM**. If you do not know this, you might think that Jesus Christ just sprung up from nowhere and was making all the outrageous statements and claims about Himself. The dictionary defines **Wisdom** as follows:

> *"Wisdom is a deep understanding and realization of people, things, events or situations, resulting in the ability to choose or act or inspire to consistently produce the optimum results with a minimum of time, energy or thought. It is the ability to optimally (effectively and efficiently) apply perceptions and knowledge and so produce the desired results.*
>
> ***Wisdom*** *is also the comprehension of what is true or right coupled with optimum judgment as to action."*

To simplify it, I would say that **Wisdom** <u>is the ability to know or determine what is true, right, and lasting.</u> It is also an insightful or a wise disposition, plan, or strategy. In other words, wisdom means having common sense or good judgment.

How Do We know that Jesus is WISDOM?

Take a look at **1 Corinthians 1:23-30**. In it, you will see the Lord revealed to us as **WISDOM:**

> "But we preach Christ crucified, unto the Jews a stumbling block, and unto the Greeks foolishness; 24 But unto them which are called, both Jews and Greeks, **Christ the power of God,**

and the <u>wisdom</u> of God... *30* But of him are ye in **Christ Jesus, who of God is made unto us** <u>wisdom</u>, and <u>righteousness</u>, and <u>sanctification</u>, and <u>redemption</u>..."

And also in the following scriptures:

"In whom are hid all the treasures of <u>wisdom</u> and <u>knowledge</u>" (Colossians 2:3).

"For it pleased the Father that **in him should all fulness dwell**; *20* And, having made peace through the blood of his cross, by him to reconcile all things unto himself; by him, I say, whether they be things in earth, or things in heaven" (Colossians 1:19-20).

In **Proverbs 8:22-31**, the Lord Jesus as **WISDOM** *(the wise and insightful side of God)*, is telling us about Himself and about how He was always with God the Father in eternity:

<u>"**The LORD possessed** me *(Wisdom)* **in the beginning of his way, before his works of old**</u>. *23* **I was set up from everlasting, from the beginning, or ever the earth was.** *24* <u>When there were no depths, **I was brought forth**; when there were no fountains abounding with water.</u> *25* **Before the mountains were settled, before the hills was I brought forth:**

26 <u>**While as yet he had not made the earth, nor the fields, nor the highest part of the dust of the world.**</u> *27* <u>**When he prepared the heavens, I was there:**</u> when he set a compass upon the face of the depth: *28* When he established the clouds above: when he strengthened the fountains of the deep:

29 When he gave to the sea his decree, that the waters should not pass his commandment: when he appointed the foundations of the earth: *30* **Then I was by him, as one brought up with him: and I was daily his delight, rejoicing always before him;** *31* Rejoicing in the **habitable** part of his earth; and **my delights were with the sons of men**..."

We see from the scriptures above that **the Lord Jesus has always been with and a part of God the Father since eternity as the Wise side of God but He changed form in order to come to earth.** In other words, the Lord Jesus did not need a human body in the realm of the spirit so, He existed in eternity as the creative part of God the Father **but it was necessary for Him to take on a human form in order to come into the world to save us as stated in Hebrews 2:14-17:**

"**Forasmuch then as the children are partakers of flesh and blood, he also himself likewise took part of the same;** that through death he might destroy him that had the power of death, that is, the devil; *15* And deliver them who through fear of death were all their lifetime subject to bondage.

16 **For verily he took not on him the nature of angels; but he took on him the seed of Abraham.** *17* Wherefore in all things it behoved him to be made like unto his brethren, that he might be a merciful and faithful high priest in things pertaining to God, to make reconciliation for the sins of the people."

The Lord tells us in **Matthew 11:19** that He is **Wisdom**. We can see for ourselves what He said about Himself and about us:

"The Son of man came eating and drinking, and they say, Behold a man gluttonous, and a winebibber, a friend of publicans and sinners. **But <u>wisdom</u>** *(meaning Himself)* **is justified of her children** *(the believers)*."

True to His word, we that are Christians are now the ones who testify today that the Lord Jesus is who He claimed to be because we are His children. As Wisdom, He was one with the Father. **So, being the children of Jesus Christ, we are therefore, the children of WISDOM.** As wisdom, the Lord has always been passionate towards mankind and He has always been everywhere speaking to humanity in His attempt to turn humanity back to God. If you look at **Proverbs 8:1-12**, you will see the Lord as **WISDOM** (the wise and insightful side of God) speaking to mankind:

"Doth not **wisdom** cry?... Unto you, O men, I call; and my voice is to the sons of man. 5 O ye simple, understand **wisdom**: and, ye fools, be ye of an understanding heart. 6 Hear; for I will speak of excellent things; and the opening of my lips shall be right things. 7 **For my mouth shall speak truth; and wickedness is an abomination to my lips**. 8 All the words of my mouth are in righteousness; there is nothing froward or perverse in them.

9 They are all plain to him that understandeth, and right to them that find knowledge *(the Jews are supposed to be the custodians of the law and they are supposed to know these scriptures and wisdom is saying here that really; if you seek understanding, wisdom should make itself plain to you).* 10 <u>Receive my instruction, and not silver; and knowledge rather than choice gold.</u>

11 For **wisdom** is better than rubies; and all the things that may be desired are not to be

compared to it. *(one of the problems in the world today is that people do not know Jesus because they are so busy pursuing material things such as gold and silver; that dollar and what that dollar can put on their table. What wisdom is saying here is wait a minute; I am more precious and more costly than anything you think is precious and of high value on earth. Truly, Jesus is more precious than anything that this world has to offer). 12* **I wisdom dwell with prudence**, and find out knowledge of witty inventions..."

Wisdom and prudence go together because once you understand the application of knowledge (wisdom); prudence tells you how to behave. As a result, you not only have the insight or understanding that you need, you also know how you are to actually behave yourself in a very wise way to get what you are looking for. **This is why wisdom and prudence go hand in hand. Jesus was always Wisdom before He became the Son of God and His desire has always been to help mankind gain insights into the ways of God so that we can experiences the true riches of God** as we see in **Proverbs 8:18-21**:

> **"Riches and honour are with me; yea, durable riches and righteousness.** *19* **My fruit is better than gold, yea, than fine gold; and my revenue than choice silver.** *20* **I lead in the way of righteousness, in the midst of the paths of judgment:** *21* That I may cause those that love me to inherit substance; and I will fill their treasures..."

As you can see, **you do not actually get God's true wealth and riches until wisdom guides you into the ways of God.** For example, there are some people who won millions and millions of dollars or come into a lot of money and then turned around and lost them all because they had no wisdom when they came into all that money. When wisdom helps you build wealth, it becomes lasting wealth. The Lord Jesus is the WISDOM that you should pursue because in Him alone will you find true riches and wealth.

It is possible to gain the riches of the world and lose your soul if you do it through unscrupulous and ungodly ways or at the expense of your soul. The Lord Jesus as Wisdom saves our souls and He blesses us with God's abundant riches and wealth. This is why He asked in **Mark 8:36-37:**

> **"For what shall it profit a man, if he shall gain the whole world, and lose his own soul? 37 Or what shall a man give in exchange for his soul?"**

In continuation of our discussion of who Jesus is, we are now going to take a look at the Lord Jesus as **the Angel of the LORD** in the next chapter. Remember that we are trying to have an in depth knowledge of Him.

Chapter 4
Jesus as the Angel of the LORD

At very important times in the Old Testament, there appeared a very special angel that the Bible refers to as **'a Man, an Angel of the LORD, the Angel of the LORD or the Angel of God**.' These biblical references to this particular angel by these names were to distinguish it from the other angels. When an angel from the general class of angels would appear, it was referred to as **'an Angel'**.

God the Father cannot look upon sin (Isaiah 59:2) because He is so holy that when a sinner appears before Him, the sinner will drop dead. According to Romans 3:23, **"For all have sinned and come short of the Glory of God."** Therefore, anyone who is not yet born again still has this sin nature. If you read Exodus 33:18-23, you will see the extent to which God went to hide Moses in the cleft of the Rock and at the same time cover Moses with His hand just so that Moses can see His back. He told Moss that Moses was not in a place (born again in Christ the Rock) where Moses can see His face and live. It is one of the reasons why sinners will never behold the glorious face of God the Father but in His mercy and in order to deal with sinful humanity, He delegated His Son to be the **Mediator**, the **Judge** and the **Savior** of all mankind. As a result, the Lord Jesus from the days of old has always appeared on earth as **God** or **the Angel of the LORD** to intervene in human affairs:

> "For there is one God, and **one mediator between God and men,** the man Christ Jesus" (1 Timothy 2:5).

Connecting the Angel of the LORD to the Lord Jesus

The dictionary **definition** of the Word **angel** is 'a messenger' or 'a messenger of God'. This explains why when God was talking about sending the Lord Jesus to the earth He referred to Him as 'the messenger of the covenant' in **Malachi 3:1-3:**

> "...And the **Lord, whom ye seek,** shall suddenly come to his temple, <u>even the messenger of the covenant</u> *(Jesus and the New Testament),* **whom ye delight in: behold, he** *(the Lord Jesus)* **shall come, saith the LORD of hosts.**
>
> 2 **But who may abide the day of his coming? and who shall stand when he appeareth? for he is like a refiner's fire, and like fullers' soap:** 3 **And he shall sit as a refiner and purifier of silver: and he shall purify the sons of Levi, and purge them as gold and silver,** that they may offer unto the LORD an offering in righteousness."

In the above scripture passage, God the Father is talking about sending His Son Jesus as the **messenger of the covenant;** meaning the **New Testament** that He established with His own blood. The reason is because God the Father has given all creation to His Son Jesus Christ and He also made Him the **LORD, Savoir, Judge,** etc., of all humanity. We are told this in **Hebrews 2:8-13** that God has put all things under the feet of the Lord Jesus and that He has crowned Him with glory and honor:

> "**Thou hast put all things in subjection under his feet. For in that he put all in subjection under him, he left nothing that is not put under him.** But now we see not yet all things put under him. 9 **But we see Jesus, who was made a little lower than the angels for the suffering of death, crowned with glory and honour;** that he by the grace of God should taste death for every man.

10 **For it became him, <u>for whom are all things,</u> and <u>by whom are all things,</u> in bringing many sons unto glory, to make the captain of their salvation perfect through sufferings.** *11* For both he that sanctifieth and they who are sanctified are all of one: for which cause he is not ashamed to call them brethren, *12* Saying, I will declare thy name unto my brethren, in the midst of the church will I sing praise unto thee. *13* And again, I will put my trust in him. And again, Behold I and the children which God hath given me."

This scripture confirms that God the Father created all things by His Son Jesus Christ *(the Word)* and He made all things for Him as well. **All of creation is one giant gift from a loving Father to His faithful and devoted Son.** He has set His Son to be the head of all of His creation as we see in **Ephesians 1:19-23:**

"And what is the exceeding greatness of his power to us-ward who believe, <u>according to the working of his mighty power,</u> *20* <u>Which he wrought in Christ, when he raised him from the dead, and set him at his own right hand in the heavenly places,</u>

21 **<u>Far above all principality,</u> and <u>power,</u> and <u>might,</u> and <u>dominion,</u> and <u>every name that is named,</u> not only in this world, but also in that which is to come:** *22* **<u>And hath put all things under his feet, and gave him to be the head over all things to the church,</u>** *23* **<u>Which is his body, the fullness of him that filleth all in all</u>**."

The Angel of the LORD Appeared to People as God

The Lord Jesus has always been the part of the Godhead

dealing with humanity since man fell into sin. This is why it was necessary for Him to appear on the human scene as **the Angel of the LORD** at times. **He has been the one having dealings with us on earth in God's stead or better put, as God.** The following scripture in **Isaiah 63:8-10** shows us the Lord Jesus' connection to the **Angel of the LORD**:

> "For he said, Surely they are my people, children that will not lie: **so he was their Saviour. 9 In all their affliction he was afflicted, and the angel of his presence saved them**: in his love and in his pity he redeemed them; and **he bare them, and carried them all the days of old** *(through the wilderness).* 10 But they rebelled, and vexed his holy Spirit..."

Also, below is the scriptural account of how the Lord Jesus was sent as **the Angel of the LORD** by God the Father to lead the children of Israel out of Egypt and through the wilderness in **Exodus 23:20-24**:

> "**Behold, I send an Angel before thee, to keep thee in the way, and to bring thee into the place which I have prepared.** 21 **Beware of him, and obey his voice, provoke him not; for he will not pardon your transgressions: for my name is in him** *(He is God).* 22 But if thou shalt indeed obey his voice, and do all that I speak; then I will be an enemy unto thine enemies, and an adversary unto thine adversaries.

> 23 **For mine Angel** *(meaning Himself)* **shall go before thee, and bring thee in unto the Amorites, and the Hittites, and the Perizzites, and the Canaanites, the Hivites, and the Jebusites: and I will cut them off.** 24 Thou shalt not bow down to their gods, nor serve them, nor do after their

works: but thou shalt utterly overthrow them, and quite break down their images."

Clearly, this particular **Angel** is called by God's name; meaning that He is God Himself. **There is another scripture in 1 Chronicles 21:15 that shows that the Lord Jesus and the Angel of the LORD are one and the same person.** The Lord was so displeased with the children of Israel that He decided to destroy Jerusalem. As a result, we see **an angel** being sent by God from the general class of angels to destroy Jerusalem and this angel is referred to as **an angel** and we also see the Lord Himself standing by on the scene as **the Angel of the LORD** as He watched the angel that He sent to destroy Jerusalem at work:

> "And God sent **an angel** unto Jerusalem to destroy it: and as he was destroying, the LORD beheld, and he repented him of the evil, and said to the angel that destroyed, It is enough, stay now thine hand. And **the Angel of the LORD** stood by the threshingfloor of Ornan the Jebusite (*the Lord Himself was present and watching as the angel was destroying Jerusalem*)."

The Angel of the LORD Speaks as God

Again, when the Bible talks about 'an Angel of the LORD, the Angel of the LORD or the Angel of God,' it is not talking about the other angels **but about this particular being that speaks and functions differently from all the other angels. This angel does not bring messages from God but speaks as God!** Below is an example in **Judges 2:1**:

> "And **an angel of the LORD** came up from Gilgal to Bochim, and said, **I made you to go up out of Egypt, and have brought you unto the land which I sware unto your fathers;**

and I said, I will never break my covenant with you."

I will like to reiterate that angels from **the general class of angels** usually bring the Word of the Lord to humans and as such, they speak <u>on behalf of God</u>. Therefore, the most interesting thing about this particular **Angel** is that He speaks as God and not on behalf of God. Take a look at what He said to Hagar; Sarah's Egyptian maidservant as she was running away from Sarai (Sarah) her mistress in **Genesis 16:7-13:**

> "And **the Angel of the LORD** found her by a fountain of water in the wilderness, by the fountain in the way to Shur. *8* And he said, Hagar, Sarai's maid, whence camest thou? and whither wilt thou go? And she said, I flee from the face of my mistress Sarai. *9* And **the Angel of the LORD** said unto her, Return to thy mistress, and submit thyself under her hands.
>
> *10* **And the Angel of the LORD said unto her, <u>I will</u> multiply thy seed exceedingly, that it shall not be numbered for multitude.** *11* And **the Angel of the LORD** said unto her, Behold, thou art with child, and shalt bear a son, and shalt call his name Ishmael; because the LORD hath heard thy affliction.
>
> *12* And he will be a wild man; his hand will be against every man, and every man's hand against him; and he shall dwell in the presence of all his brethren. *13* **And she called the name of the LORD that spake unto her, Thou God seest me**: for she said, Have I also here looked after him that seeth me?"

The Angel of the LORD Receives Worship
When you read Old Testament writings, you will notice that this particular angel; <u>the Angel of the LORD receives</u>

worship and those who address Him, call Him LORD and He does not rebuke them because He is both LORD and God! Below is an account of how **the Angel of the LORD** received worship from Gideon in **Judges 6:11-24:**

"And there came **an angel of the LORD,** and sat under an oak which was in Ophrah, that pertained unto Joash the Abiezrite: and his son Gideon threshed wheat by the winepress, to hide it from the Midianites. *12* And **the Angel of the LORD** appeared unto him, and said unto him, The LORD is with thee, thou mighty man ol valour.

13 And Gideon said unto him, **Oh my Lord,** if the LORD be with us, why then is all this befallen us? and where be all his miracles which our fathers told us of, saying, Did not the LORD bring us up from Egypt? but now the LORD hath forsaken us, and delivered us into the hands of the Midianites. *14* **And the LORD looked upon him,** and said, Go in this thy might, and thou shalt save Israel from the hand of the Midianites: **have not I sent thee**? *(He speaks as God).*

15 And he said unto him, Oh my Lord, wherewith shall I save Israel? behold, my family is poor in Manasseh, and I am the least in my father's house. *16* **And the LORD said unto him, Surely I will be with thee, and thou shalt smite the Midianites as one man.** *17* And he said unto him, If now I have found grace in thy sight, then shew me a sign that thou talkest with me.

18 Depart not hence, I pray thee, until I come unto thee, and bring forth my present, and set it before thee. And he said, I will tarry until thou come again. *19* And Gideon went in, and made ready a kid, and unleavened cakes of an ephah of flour: the flesh he put in a basket, and he put the broth in a pot, and brought it out unto him under the oak, and presented it.

20 And **the angel of God** said unto him, <u>Take the flesh and the unleavened cakes, and lay them upon this rock, and pour out the broth. And he did so</u>. 21 Then **the Angel of the LORD** put forth the end of the staff that was in his hand, and touched the flesh and the unleavened cakes; and there rose up fire out of the rock, and consumed the flesh and the unleavened cakes. **Then the Angel of the LORD departed out of his sight.**

22 <u>**And when Gideon perceived that he was an angel of the LORD, Gideon said, Alas, O Lord GOD!**</u> **for because I have seen an angel of the LORD face to face.** 23 <u>**And the LORD said unto him**</u>**, Peace be unto thee; fear not: thou shalt not die.** 24 Then Gideon built an altar there unto the LORD, and called it *Jehovah shalom...*"

It is obvious in the above scripture that **"the Angel of the LORD or the Angel of God"** can receive worship and **it is an act of treason for any other angel to receive worship.** Seeking and receiving worship (self-idolatry) was the sin that Lucifer committed as recorded in **Isaiah 14:12-15.** He was an Archangel but he wanted to receive the worship that only God can receive and by doing this, God said that he had sinned. Therefore, God judged and abased him and He also stripped him of all the glory and status that he once enjoyed as an Archangel. Today, he is nothing but an evil spirit:

"How art thou fallen from heaven, **O Lucifer, son of the morning!** how art thou cut down to the ground, which didst weaken the nations!

13 For thou hast said in thine heart, I will ascend into heaven, I will exalt my throne above the stars of God: I will sit <u>also</u> upon the mount of <u>the congregation</u> (*God sits as the head of all the congregations that worship Him*)**, in the sides of the north: 14 I will ascend above the heights of the clouds; I will be like the most High.** 15 Yet thou shalt be brought down to hell, to the sides of the pit."

God made Lucifer an example of what happens to those who seek to take God's glory (worship and adoration) by stripping him of all that God had previously given him and also, by reducing him to a caricature of a being. In other words, God made him an aberration for all ages and he is now only suited for one thing — to be destroyed at a set time!

After the fall or abasement of Lucifer, no angel will dare to receive worship because every angel knows that worship and adoration belong only to God. This is the whole problem that God has with humanity; the making and the worshipping of idols. Since his fall, the devil is quick to get people to worship anything else but the One True God because he knows that it is the quickest way to earn God's wrath and abasement. As a result, angels are quick to correct those who try to worship them. A very good example is found in **Revelation 22:8-9:**

"And I John saw these things, and heard them. <u>And when I had heard and seen, I fell down</u> **<u>to worship before the feet of the angel</u>** which shewed me these things. 9 <u>Then saith he unto me,</u> **See thou do it not:** for I am thy fellow servant, and of thy brethren the prophets, and of them which keep the sayings of this book: **<u>worship God</u>**."

Our God is a jealous God as He told us in **Exodus 34:14;** He will not share His glory (adoration, worship, reverence, acceptance of offering, etc.) with any other entity including His angels. Therefore we must be careful to give Him all our worship:

> "For thou shalt worship no other god: **for the LORD, whose name is Jealous, is a jealous God**..."

The Angel of the LORD is a Warrior

The Lord is a warrior and the Bible calls Him the 'Man of War' in **Exodus 15:3:**

> "**The LORD is a man of war:** the LORD is his name."

At different times as the children of Israel journeyed through the wilderness and even after God had settled them in the land of Canaan, **the Angel of the LORD** went to the camp of Israel's enemies and single handedly slew their enemies. The scripture in **2 Kings 19:35** gives us a very good example of this:

> "**And it came to pass that night, that the <u>angel of the LORD</u> went out, and smote in the camp of the <u>Assyrians</u> an hundred fourscore and five thousand:** and when they arose early in the morning, behold, they were all dead corpses."

Also, when the Lord saw that the Prophet Balaam was perverse when it came to money, gifts and honor, He came down as **the Angel of the LORD** to confront Balaam. He went out against Balaam as we see in **Numbers 22:23-32:**

> "**And the ass saw <u>the angel of the LORD</u> standing in the way, and his sword drawn in**

his hand: and the ass turned aside out of the way, and went into the field: and Balaam smote the ass, to turn her into the way. 24 But the angel of the LORD stood in a path of the vineyards, a wall being on this side, and a wall on that side.

25 And when the ass saw **the angel of the LORD,** she thrust herself unto the wall, and crushed Balaam's foot against the wall: and he smote her again… 31 **Then the LORD opened the eyes of Balaam, and he saw the angel of the LORD standing in the way, and his sword drawn in his hand:** and he *(Balaam)* bowed down his head, and fell flat on his face.

32 And **the angel of the LORD** said unto him, Wherefore hast thou smitten thine ass these three times? **behold, I went out to withstand thee, because thy way is perverse before me …**"

Clearly He spoke to Balaam as God and not on behalf of God. As God, He can judge Balaam and He did.

In the days of King David, the Lord was so angry with the children of Israel that He came down as **the Angel of the LORD** to personally destroy Jerusalem as recorded in **1 Chronicles 21-16:**

> **"And David lifted up his eyes, and saw the angel of the LORD stand between the earth and the heaven, having a drawn sword in his hand stretched out over Jerusalem.** Then David and the elders of Israel, who were clothed in sackcloth, fell upon their faces…"

King David and the elders of Israel had to intercede and beg God for forgivness. Also, on several occasions, King

David cried out to the Lord as the **'Man of War'** asking for His intervention against his enemies as we see in **Psalm 35:1-6:**

> **"Plead my cause, O LORD, with them that strive with me: fight against them that fight against me.** 2 Take hold of shield and buckler, and stand up for mine help. 3 **Draw out also the spear, and stop the way against them that persecute me**: say unto my soul, I am thy salvation.
>
> 4 Let them be confounded and put to shame that seek after my soul: let them be turned back and brought to confusion that devise my hurt. 5 **Let them be as chaff before the wind: and let** the <u>angel of the LORD</u> **chase them.** 6 **Let their way be dark and slippery: and let** <u>the angel of the LORD</u> **persecute them."**

The Angel of the LORD actually protects all those who place their trust in the Lord. He defends all those who belong to God according to **Psalm 34:7:**

> **"**<u>The angel of the LORD</u> **encampeth round about them that fear him, and delivereth them."**

The Angel of the LORD Appeared to Abraham

When God the Father was ready to bring forth His plan of salvation for mankind, He looked for a man on earth and He found that man in Abraham. First, He subjected Abraham to a very long period of waiting to have a son. He did this to make sure that the child will be Abraham's well beloved son.

God demanded that Abraham sacrifice his well beloved Isaac that he waited over 25 years to have! Abraham obeyed God by taking his well beloved son Isaac to Mount Moriah to sacrifice him but when Abraham raised his knife to deal Isaac a deadly stab, the Lord showed up on the scene as **the Angel of the LORD** in **Genesis 22:2-12:**

> "And he said, Take now thy son, thine only son Isaac, whom thou lovest, and get thee into the land of Moriah; and offer him there for a burnt offering upon one of the mountains which I will tell thee of… 10 <u>And Abraham stretched forth his hand, and took the knife to slay his son.</u> 11 **And <u>the Angel of the LORD</u> called unto him out of heaven, and said, Abraham, Abraham:** and he said, Here am I. 12 And he said, **Lay not thine hand upon the lad, neither do thou anything unto him: for <u>now I know</u> that thou fearest God, seeing thou hast not withheld thy son, thine only son <u>from me</u>…**"

The Angel of the LORD Spoke to Jacob as God

We also see Jacob's account of his encounter with **the Angel of God** in **Genesis 31:11-13.** Jacob fled to Padanaram in order to escape the wrath of his brother Esau whose birthright he stole before the death of their father Isaac. On the way to Padanaram, he had an encounter with **the Angel of the LORD** in Bethel.

After many years, Jacob successfully established a family with two wives and children but he was still working for his father in-law Laban. Although Jacob had been very cunning and crafty, Laban proved to be even more so. This was demonstrated by the fact that although Jacob was a family man in his own right, his father in-law was still misusing him to his own advantage and was undermining his status. As a result, Jacob served Laban for over 14 years and Laban paid him miserable wages.

Therefore, Jacob needed to devise a plan to outwit Laban's plans against him. When he came up with a plan, God helped him out because God saw that Laban had been very unfair to him as we see in **Genesis 31:11-13:**

"And **the angel of God** **spake unto me in a dream,** saying, Jacob: And I said, Here am I. 12 And he said, Lift up now thine eyes, and see, all the rams which leap upon the cattle are ringstraked, speckled, and grisled: **for I have seen all that Laban doeth unto thee**. 13 **I am the God of Bethel, where thou anointedst the pillar, and where thou vowedst a vow unto me**: now arise, get thee out from this land, and return unto the land of thy kindred..."

In this scripture above, **the Angel of the LORD** referred to Himself as **God**.

The Angel of the LORD Wrestled with Jacob

We have already seen that the Lord Jesus is the part of the Godhead that appears in the Old Testament as **the Angel of the LORD** to deal with human beings directly on earth. As **the Angel of the LORD**, He took on the appearance of a man but His name was hidden. The reason for this was because God the Father wanted His Son's name revealed at His appointed time for the salvation of humanity –*"For there is none other name under heaven given among men, whereby we must be saved"* **(Acts 4:12)**. Jacob wanted to know His name when He visited Jacob and they wrestled throughout the night. This encounter is recorded in **Genesis 32:24-30:**

"And Jacob was left alone; **and there wrestled a man with him until the breaking of the day.** 25 And when he saw that he prevailed not against him, he touched the hollow of his thigh; and the hollow of Jacob's thigh was out of joint, as he wrestled with him.

26 And he said, Let me go, for the day breaketh. And he said, I will not let thee go except thou bless me. *27* And he said unto him, What is thy name? And he said, Jacob. *28* <u>And he said, Thy name shall be called no more Jacob, but Israel</u>: **for as a prince <u>hast thou power with God</u> and with men, and hast prevailed**.

29 <u>And Jacob asked him, and said, Tell me, I pray thee, thy name</u>. **And he said, Wherefore is it that thou dost ask after my name?** <u>And he blessed him there</u>. *30* <u>And Jacob called the name of the place Peniel</u>: **for I have seen God face to face, and my life is preserved**."

As **the Angel of the LORD** (a man), the Lord blessed Jacob before He quickly disappeared as Jacob was pressing Him for His identity. Before His manifestation as the Son of God on earth, the Lord' name; **JESUS** or **YESHUA** was one of heaven's most hidden secrets. When combined with **CHRIST** (anointed), it becomes heaven's most deadly arsenal! This is why we are to use the name of **Jesus Christ** to cast out devils, heal the sick, raise the dead, and preach the Gospel in order to bring about the salvation of souls.

The Angel of the LORD Appeared to Moses as God

The Lord Jesus appeared unto Moses as **the Angel of the LORD** in the burning bush in **Exodus 3:2-6:**

"**And <u>the Angel of the LORD</u> appeared unto him in a flame of fire out of the midst of a bush:** and he looked, and, behold, the bush burned with fire, and the bush was not consumed. *3* And Moses said, I will now turn aside, and see this great sight, why the bush is not burnt.

4 And when the LORD saw that he turned aside to see, God called unto him out of the midst of the bush, and said, Moses, Moses. And he said, Here am I. 5 And he said, Draw not nigh hither: put off thy shoes from off thy feet, for the place where on thou standest is holy ground.

6 Moreover he said, **I am the God of thy father,** the God of Abraham, the God of Isaac, and the God of Jacob. And Moses hid his face; for he was afraid to look upon God."

In the above scripture, you see the Lord Jesus using three of His names: **the Angel of the LORD, the LORD,** and **God**! He has always been interacting with mankind since God created Adam and Adam fell into sin.

In the above passage from **Exodus**, you see the Lord Jesus as **the Angel of the LORD** talking to Moses and introducing Himself to Moses. As I stated in the first of these three book series titled: *Experiencing the Depths of God the Father (Chapter 2, page 27),* Moses came on the scene totally ignorant of who God was but out of curiosity, he had an encounter with God by the burning bush and this began his relationship with God. Below is an excerpt:

"Moses was not particularly a religious person as defined by the Jewish customs of his days because he grew up in the house of Pharaoh and he was instructed in all the ways of Egypt. He knew all the Egyptian ways of worship and customs but the God of Abraham, Isaac and Jacob was unknown to him. He was actually minding his own business in the woods when he suddenly saw a bush burning and he went to check it out.

He was amazed at the fact that the bush was burning but it was not being consumed so his curiosity got the best of *him and he went to investigate it. The Bible says that <u>when God saw that Moses turned aside to look at the bush</u>, God spoke to him as recorded above."*

Today, we know that it was the Lord Jesus that met Moses at the burning bush as **the Angel of the LORD**. Therefore, as you can clearly see, the Lord Jesus did not just appear on the scene from nowhere. It is just that people did not know who He was when they began to encounter Him and as a result, they ruled Him out because their belief was that nothing good had ever come out of Galilee.

Although the High Priest said that people should check and see if there had ever been any prophet out of Galilee, neither him nor the other priests ever bothered to check out the Lord Jesus' genealogy. This in itself was tragic because if there was a nation that kept good and accurate birth records in those days, it was the Jewish nation. It was a gross negligence and a serious mistake on their part to just take a look at the Lord Jesus and dismiss Him as not being who He said He was.

Just as in the days of the Jewish leaders, there are people today that do not want to take the time to find out about who the Lord Jesus really is and about His message of salvation for all mankind. What they fail to realize is that He is the only way to God the Father. There is no other way. It is the reason He said so emphatically in **John 14:6:**

> "**...I am the way, the truth,** and **the life: no man cometh unto the Father, <u>but by me</u>.**"

Remember that when Jesus was about to be born, Joseph and Mary had to go to Bethlehem so that they can be recorded because there was a national census going on? God did not leave Jesus without any testimony of who He was. Any search of the Jewish records would have revealed that He was right out of the house of David

because Jacob prophesied that the scepter would come out of the tribe of Judah.

As a result of the prophecy that said that the Sceptre will not depart from Judah in **Genesis 49:10**, all the Jews knew that the **Messiah** was going to come out of the tribe of Judah:

> "**The sceptre shall not depart from Judah, nor a lawgiver from between his feet, until Shiloh** *(Shiloh is the Messianic name of the Lord Jesus)* **come**; and unto him shall the gathering of the people be."

The mistake they made was that they expected the **Messiah** to come maybe with the moon and the stars following Him to help announce to everyone that He was the Messiah. Instead, He came according to the Word of the Lord; "wanting to be like His brethren" and with the humblest of all births; the stables where animals are kept! Even this was prophetic because He was going to be a lamb to be sacrificed. The Lord Jesus' physical appearance was not different from any other normal Jewish man so that when they came to arrest Him, they needed Judas' help to identify Him from His disciples because you could not tell Him apart from His brethren.

He did not come into the world with any outward distinctions or manifestations on His person or body that made him to stand out from everyone else. Rather, He came to blend in and that He did very well. He was not like some of us that think that because God has given us a 'big ministry' we can go around all puffed up. Today, there are some ministers that you cannot get an audience with because they have a 'big ministry'. Actually, you have a better chance of seeing the President of the United States than seeing them. Even when you meet them, they are too puffed up to be of any use as God's vehicles of love but it was not so with the Lord Jesus. He was accessible and He freely mingled among ordinary people; even among those that society had rejected.

In other words, He dwelt among the people and He did not place Himself out of the reach of those who wanted to have an encounter with Him.

The Angel of the LORD Appeared to Manoah and His Wife

Manoah and his wife were the parents of Samson. Samson was one of the **Judges** that ruled Israel before kings began to reign in Israel. At this time in the Jewish history, God wanted to send His hand-picked man to rule Israel and to deliver Israel from the hands of the Philistines. He chose Manoah and his wife to be the parents of the **child that would become the deliver and the Judge** and He wanted to give them specific instructions on how to raise the child.

Therefore, He showed up on the scene of their lives as **the Angel of the LORD.** Here is an account of the interaction between **the Angel of the LORD** and Samson's parents in **Judges 13:1-6**:

> "And the children of Israel did evil again in the sight of the LORD; and the LORD delivered them into the hand of the Philistines forty years. 2 And there was a certain man of Zorah, of the family of the Danites, whose name was Manoah; and his wife was barren, and bare not.
>
> 3 And **the Angel of the LORD appeared unto the woman,** and said unto her, Behold now, thou art barren, and bearest not: but thou shalt conceive, and bear a son. 4 Now therefore beware, I pray thee, and drink not wine nor strong drink, and eat not any unclean thing:
>
> 5 For, lo, thou shalt conceive, and bear a son; and no razor shall come on his head: for the child shall be a Nazarite unto God from the

womb: and he shall begin to deliver Israel out of the hand of the Philistines. *6* Then the woman came and told her husband, saying, **A man of God** came unto me, **and his countenance was like the countenance of <u>an angel of God</u>, very terrible**: but I asked him not whence he was, neither told he me his name..."

Also, **Judges 13:15-18** is a record of what happened when Samson's father, Manoah in ignorance asked **the Angel of the LORD** His name. What Manoah did not know was that at this time in God's dealing with mankind; the Lord's name (**Yeshua Hamashiach or Jesus Christ**) was top secret:

> "**And Manoah said unto <u>the Angel of the LORD</u>,** I pray thee, let us detain thee, until we shall have made ready a kid for thee. *16* And **the Angel of the LORD** said unto Manoah, Though thou detain me, I will not eat of thy bread: and if thou wilt offer a burnt offering, thou must offer it unto the LORD.

> **For Manoah knew not that <u>he was an angel of the LORD</u>** *(He wanted Manoah to honor Him as Lord).* *17* **And Manoah said unto <u>the Angel of the LORD</u>, What is thy name, that when thy sayings come to pass we may do thee honour?** *18* And **the Angel of the LORD** said unto him, **Why askest thou thus after my name, seeing it is secret?**"

We have seen that the Lord Jesus functioned as **the Angel of the LORD or the Angel of God** and even sometimes as **a Man** in the Old Testament. The reason for this is because from time to time, He came down from heaven to intervene in our earthly situations and circumstances. **Ever since He was manifested on earth and His identity revealed as the Lord**

Jesus Christ, He no longer keeps His name and identity <u>secret</u> when He appears as <u>the Angel of the LORD.</u>

Now, He can announce Himself as the Lord (Angel of the Lord) because His **name and identity are now in the Public Domain for all Christians to call on or use in the time of trouble.** Also, we can now know Him and we can reverently call Him by His name. He is still available to help us in all of our earthly situations.

The Angel of the LORD Appeared in the New Testament

The Angel of the LORD also appeared in the New Testament to Cornelius as he was fasting and praying in **Acts 10:1-6:**

> "There was a certain man in Caesarea called Cornelius, a centurion of the band called the Italian band, 2 A devout man, and one that feared God with all his house, which gave much alms to the people, and prayed to God alway. 3 He saw in a vision evidently about the ninth hour of the day **an angel of God** coming in to him, and saying unto him, Cornelius.
>
> 4 <u>And when he looked on him, he was afraid, and said,</u> **What is it, Lord?** And he said unto him, **Thy prayers and thine alms are come up for a memorial before God.** 5 And now send men to Joppa, and call for one Simon, whose surname is Peter: 6 He lodgeth with one Simon a tanner, whose house is by the sea side: he shall tell thee what thou oughtest to do."

We see here that **<u>the Angel of the LORD</u>** did not rebuke Cornelius for calling Him **Lord** because it was the Lord

Himself. Today, as a born again Christian when I need His intervention as **the Angel of the LORD**, I call on the Lord as follows:

*"As it is written in **Psalm 35**, Lord Jesus, I ask that You arise as **the Angel of the LORD** and contend with them that contend with me, persecute all the evil spirits that are persecuting me and fight against them that fight against me. In Your Name, I speak destruction to their plans against me."*

And also,

*"Father, thank You that Your Son, my Lord Jesus Christ as **the Angel of the LORD** is warring on my behalf in this situation as it is written:*

*'... **And in righteousness he doth judge and make war'** (Revelation 19:11).*

*Thank you Father, for answering my prayer and for sending **the Angel of the LORD** to war on my behalf in Jesus Name."*

Chapter 5
Jesus as the LORD of Hosts and Captain of the LORD's Hosts

Just as He is the **"the Angel of the LORD,"** the Lord Jesus is also referred to as the **LORD of Hosts** or as **the Captain of the LORD's Hosts.** What this means is that before He took on the form of a man and came to the earth as Jesus the Christ, He operated as **the LORD of Hosts or as Captain of the LORD's Hosts.**

He adorns these titles when He is going to war or is present to help in times when we need His deliverance. We see Him standing as such before Joshua in Gilgal in the plains of Jericho in **Joshua 5:13-15:**

> "And it came to pass, when Joshua was by Jericho, that he lifted up his eyes and looked, and, behold, **there stood a man over against him with his sword drawn in his hand:** and Joshua went unto him, and said unto him, Art thou for us, or for our adversaries?
>
> 14 **And he said, Nay; but as** captain of the host of the LORD **am I now come.** And Joshua fell on his face to the earth, and did worship, and said unto him, **What saith** my lord **unto his servant?** 15 **And** the captain of the LORD'S host **said unto Joshua, Loose thy shoe from off thy foot; for the place whereon thou standest is holy.** And Joshua did so."

Whenever the children of Israel placed their trust in Him instead of idols, He was always present to defend them. Also, when we want Him to defend and war on our behalf today as His Church, we must know and refer to Him as the **LORD**

of Hosts or as the Captain of the LORD's Hosts. Again, He is the part of the Godhead that appears as **"a man"** in time of war to help all those who place their trust in God. Christians who are in the military forces need to know this as they head out to the warfront so that they can call on Him.

It was the **LORD of Hosts** that helped David to defeat Goliath the giant. Goliath cursed David by his gods and David invoked the name of **the LORD of Hosts** against Goliath before David charged against him. Because **the LORD of Hosts** is "a Man of War," He helped David to take out Goliath as recorded in **1 Samuel 17:42-46:**

> "And when the Philistine *(Goliath)* looked about, and saw David, he disdained him: for he was but a youth, and ruddy, and of a fair countenance. 43 And the Philistine said unto David, Am I a dog, that thou comest to me with staves? And the Philistine cursed David by his gods. 44 And the Philistine said to David, Come to me, and I will give thy flesh unto the fowls of the air, and to the beasts of the field.
>
> 45 Then said David to the Philistine, **Thou comest to me with a sword, and with a spear, and with a shield: but I come to thee in the name of the LORD of hosts, the God of the armies of Israel, whom thou hast defied. 46 This day will the LORD deliver thee into mine hand**; and I will smite thee, and take thine head from thee; and I will give the carcases of the host of the Philistines this day unto the fowls of the air, and to the wild beasts of the earth; **that all the earth may know that there is a God in Israel."**

What is most interesting about the Lord Jesus as **the LORD of Hosts** today is that He can now take on the form of any normal man and appear to people to help them in their times of need without them knowing that it is Him. **He can help and be gone and the people will think that a regular person showed up from nowhere to help them because He now has a glorified body that He can <u>make to look like any one of us</u> when He comes into the earth.** We need to learn to call on Him when we are in danger or when we are faced with dangerous enemies.

The Ark of the Covenant is called by the Name of 'the LORD of Hosts'

The children of Israel took the **Ark of the Covenant** into the battlefields to let their enemies know that God — **the LORD of Hosts** will give them victory. In other words, **the presence of the Ark of the Covenant in the battlefield meant that the LORD of Hosts was there to fight their enemies for them.**

> "And David arose, and went with all the people that were with him from Baale of Judah, to bring up from thence **the ark of God, whose name is called by the name of the LORD of hosts** that dwelleth between the cherubims" (2 Sammuel 6:2).

The enemies of the children of Israel were always very afraid of the presence of **the LORD of Hosts** in the battlefield because it meant that they will surely be defeated by the children of Israel.

The LORD of Hosts Receives Worship

We saw that **the LORD of Hosts** received Joshua's worship in **Joshua 5:15**. He commanded Joshua to take off his shoes when Joshua was standing before Him: **the LORD of Hosts**; his **God**! What this means is that His presence as **the LORD of Hosts** made the ground Holy. This is the same thing that He said to Moses in **Exodus 3:4-6**:

"And when the LORD saw that he turned aside to see, God called unto him out of the midst of the bush, and said, Moses, Moses. And he said, Here am I. 5 And he said, **Draw not nigh hither: put off thy shoes from off thy feet, for the place whereon thou standest is holy ground. 6 Moreover he said, I am the God of thy father, the God of Abraham, the God of Isaac, and the God of Jacob...**"

From these scriptures, you can see that **the LORD of Hosts** is God Himself and as God, received worship. Another example is recorded in **1 Samuel 1:3** about the man Elkanah (Hannah's husband). He went to Shiloh every year to sacrifice to **the LORD of Hosts** while Eli and his sons were still alive as the priests before the Lord:

"And this man went up out of his city yearly to worship and to sacrifice unto the **LORD of hosts** in Shiloh. And the two sons of Eli, Hophni and Phinehas, the priests of the LORD, were there."

Also, Hannah (Elkanah's barren wife) prayed to **the LORD of Hosts** while she was in desperate need to have a child. She petitioned Him to give her a son and she promised that she will in return give the child back to the Lord as recorded in **1 Samuel 1:11:**

"**And she vowed a vow, and said, O LORD of hosts, if thou wilt indeed look on the affliction of thine handmaid, and remember me, and not forget thine handmaid, but wilt give unto thine handmaid a man child, then I will give him unto the LORD all the days of his life, and there shall no razor come upon his head.**"

The LORD of Hosts answered her prayer and she conceived, and delivered a child that grew up to become the Prophet

Samuel. As the **LORD of Hosts**, the Lord Jesus was very much involved in delivering the children of Israel from their enemies, leading them to victories in wars, and granting their individual as well as their national petitions to Him.

Israel is to Cry Out to the Lord Jesus as the LORD of Hosts

The Lord Himself told the children of Israel that they will not see Him again until the day that they shall cry out for Him to come as follows in **Luke 13:35:**

> "Behold, your house is left unto you desolate·
> **and verily I say unto you, Ye shall not see me,**
> **until the time come when ye shall say, Blessed**
> **is <u>he that cometh in the name of the Lord</u>.**"

Today, we all have to call on the Lord Jesus as the one who comes in the name of the LORD God; meaning **the LORD of Hosts** to help in time of need.

Jesus Re-entered Heaven as the LORD of Hosts

The Bible tells us that after the Lord's death and resurrection, He '<u>led captivity captive</u>' and in **Psalm 24:7-10**, we see His triumphant return to heaven with Abraham and all the 'saints who slept' (the former captives of the devil in hell). He re-entered heaven as the **LORD of Hosts** and the **King of Glory** and He commanded heaven's gates and doors to open:

> "Lift up your heads, O ye gates; and be ye lift up, ye everlasting doors; and the **King of glory** shall come in. *8* **Who is this King of glory? The LORD strong and mighty, the LORD mighty in battle.** *9* Lift up your heads, O ye gates; even lift them up, ye everlasting doors; and the **King**

of glory shall come in. *10* Who is this King of glory? The **LORD of hosts**, he is the **King of glory**. Selah."

Hence the 'saints who slept' were seen coming out of the graves after His resurrection as recorded below in **Matthew 27:51-53:**

"And, behold, the veil of the temple was rent in twain from the top to the bottom; and the earth did quake, and the rocks rent; *52* **And the graves were opened; and many bodies of the saints which slept arose.** *53* And came out of the graves after his resurrection, and went into the holy city, and appeared unto many."

Chapter 6
Jesus as 'That Prophet'

God Promised to Send a Very Unique Prophet to Israel
This is recorded in **Deuteronomy 18:18-19** as follows:

> "I will raise them up a <u>Prophet</u> from among their brethren, like unto thee *(Moses)*, and will put my words in his mouth; and he shall speak unto them all that I shall command him. *19* <u>And it shall come to pass, that whosoever will not hearken unto **my words which he shall speak in my name,** I will require it of him.</u>"

As a result, since the days of Moses, the children of Israel had a great expectation for the coming of this great **Prophet** in whom the Spirit of the Lord will be upon. Moses their deliverer also emphasized the coming of this **Prophet** by repeating what God told him about this **Prophet** to the children of Israel. This happened while they were still in the wilderness in **Deuteronomy 18:15-16:**

> "The LORD thy God will raise up unto thee <u>a Prophet</u> from the midst of thee, of thy brethren, like unto me; unto him ye shall hearken; *16* According to all that thou desiredst of the LORD thy God in Horeb in the day of the assembly, saying, Let me not hear again the voice of the LORD my God, neither let me see this great fire any more, that I die not."

This is why the children of Israel expected the coming of this <u>Prophet</u> and they also knew that this <u>Prophet</u> will be their Messiah. Therefore, whenever someone came on the scene and the power of God was upon the person, they would wonder if the person was the **Prophet** that Moses talked about.

The Jews Wondered if John the Baptist was 'That Prophet'

The Jewish leaders and the Jewish people remembered God's promise to send them a special **Prophet** in the days of **John the Baptist**. Therefore, when **John the Baptist** showed up on the scene and the Spirit of the Lord began to move through him, they wondered whether or not he was this unique **Prophet** that God promised them. As a result, they sent messengers to **John the Baptist** to find out if he was **'that Prophet'** as recorded in **John 1:19-21**:

> "And this is the record of John, **when the Jews sent priests and Levites from Jerusalem to ask him, Who art thou?** 20 And he confessed, and denied not; but confessed, I am not the Christ. 21 And they asked him, **What then? Art thou Elias?** And he saith, I am not. **Art thou that prophet?** And he answered, **No**."

John the Baptist's explanation of his reply is revealed in **John 1:23**:

> "**He said, I am the voice of one crying in the wilderness, Make straight the way of the Lord**, as said the prophet Esaias."

In other words, John the Baptist told those who were questioning him that he was only sent to prepare the way for the Lord's coming. John the Baptist said again in **John 3:28-30**:

> "**Ye yourselves bear me witness, that I said, I am not the Christ, but that I am sent before him**. 29 He that hath the bride is the bridegroom: but the friend of the bridegroom, which standeth and heareth him, rejoiceth greatly because of the bridegroom's voice: this my joy therefore is fulfilled. 30 **He must increase, but I must decrease**."

Jesus as 'that Prophet' is Greater Than All the Prophets

The Lord told us in **Luke 7:26-28** that <u>of all the prophets that ever lived, John the Baptists was the greatest</u> but that even the least person in the kingdom of God (a born again Christian) is greater than John the Baptist:

> <u>"But what went ye out for to see?</u> **A prophet? Yea, I say unto you, and much more than a prophet.** 27 This is he, of whom it is written, Behold, I send my messenger before thy face, which shall prepare thy way before thee. 28 **For I say unto you, Among those that are born of women** <u>there is not a greater prophet than</u> **John the Baptist**: <u>but he that is least in the kingdom of God is greater than he."</u>

The Lord Jesus is mightier and greater than John the Baptist hence in John's testimony about the identity of the Lord Jesus, he told us that the Lord Jesus was God's Son and that Jesus was greater than him. John further testified that he (John) saw the Holy Spirit descending in the form of a Dove and resting upon the Lord and that he heard God's voice telling him about the identity of the Lord Jesus. **God actually sent John to make the Lord Jesus known to the Jews as the Messiah.** We see again in **Luke 3:15-17**, what John the Baptist said to those who were still asking him **whether or not he was the <u>Christ</u>**:

> <u>"And as the people were in expectation, and **all men mused in their hearts of John, whether he were the Christ, or not**</u>; 16 John answered, saying unto them all, I indeed baptize you with water; **but one mightier than I cometh, the latchet of whose shoes I am not worthy to unloose: he shall baptize you with the Holy Ghost and with fire:**
>
> 17 Whose fan is in his hand, and he will thoroughly purge his floor, and will gather the

wheat into his garner; but the chaff he will burn with fire unquenchable."

True to John's words, anyone who receives the Baptism of the Holy Spirit today receives it from the Lord Jesus Christ. No one else can baptize anyone with the Holy Spirit or with fire. It is the fire of the Holy Ghost that lights up the Word of God to us so that we can understand it.

Talking about greatness, the Lord also told us in His own Words in **Matthew 12:42** that He is greater than Solomon; the richest and greatest King to ever rule on earth:

> "The queen of the south shall rise up in the judgment with this generation, and shall condemn it: for she came from the uttermost parts of the earth to hear the wisdom of Solomon; **and, behold, a greater than Solomon is here.**"

Furthermore, the Lord told us that yes, John the Baptist bore witness of the fact that He (Jesus) was the Christ, but that He Himself, has an even greater witness than that of John as recorded in **John 5:33-37:**

> "**Ye sent unto John, and he bare witness unto the truth. 34 But I receive not testimony from man:** but these things I say, that ye might be saved. 35 He *(John the Baptist)* was a burning and a shining light: <u>and ye were willing for a season to rejoice in his light</u>.
>
> 36 **But I have greater witness than that of John:** <u>for the works which the Father hath given me to finish, the same works that I do, bear witness of me, that the Father hath sent me</u>. 37 **And the Father himself, which hath sent me, hath borne witness of me**. Ye have neither heard his voice at any time, nor seen his shape."

Jesus as 'that Prophet' Spoke God's Word

The scriptures above are the confirmation or the manifestation of the Word that God the Father spoke to Moses in **Deuteronomy 18:18 that He would send Israel a Prophet.** Also, according to God, this **Prophet** that He would send will speak only what He (God the Father) tells Him and He will not do His own will. The Lord Jesus also confirmed this Word of God by informing us in **John 5:30** that He does not seek His own will but that He only does the will of the Father:

> "I can of mine own self do nothing: as I hear, I judge: and my judgment is just; **because I seek not mine own will, but the will of the Father which hath sent me.**"

The Lord Jesus as **'that Prophet'** fulfilled every word that God said that the **Prophet** would do. His Spirit is also known as the **Spirit of Prophecy** because He is the head of **all Prophets** and of His **Prophetic Church.**

Chapter 7
Jesus as the Word of God

The Apostle John's Revelation about Jesus

The Apostle John was given the revelation of the identity of the Lord Jesus and he wrote the book of John. As a result of the revelation that he received concerning the Lord Jesus, he was able to explain concisely that Jesus **is the WORD of God** in **John 1:1-5**. He traced the Lord's identity to the **Book of Genesis** while explaining to the Jews about the **"Beginning;"** meaning from the time that God began to speak His Words of creation:

> **"In the beginning was the Word, and the Word was with God, and the Word was God**. 2 The same was in the beginning with God. 3 **All things were made by him**; and without him was not anything made that was made. 4 In him was life; and the life was the light of men. 5 And the light shineth in darkness; and the darkness comprehended it not."

God cannot make it any clearer that the **Lord Jesus** is **His own Word** that has always been a part of Him from the beginning. As God the Father Himself once said to me, **"You cannot separate a man from his word."** Therefore, it is no longer a mystery that the Lord Jesus is the Word that came out of God the Father's mouth.

This is also the reason why the Apostle John told us that **God created all things by Jesus Christ** in *verse 3* of the above scripture because **God speaks things into existence**. The **Book of Genesis** shows us how He creates by saying, **"Let there be..."** To see how God creates, let us take a look at the Lord Jesus (the Word of God) in the **Book of Genesis** in the subtitle below.

A Look at Jesus in Genesis Chapter One

Genesis 1:1-3 began by informing us that in the dateless past *(beginning)*, God began His work of creation as follows:

> "In the beginning **God** created the heaven and the earth. 2 And the earth was without form, and void; and darkness was upon the face of the deep. And the **Spirit of God** moved upon the face of the waters.
>
> 3 **And God said** *(the WORD)*, Let there be light: and there was light. 4 And God saw the light, that it was good: and God divided the light from the darkness..."

As you just saw in the above scripture, **the Trinity or the Godhead was at work** —God the Father, God the Son *(the Word)* and God the Holy Spirit. **They all got involved in creation because God the Father speaks or makes a decree and by the power of His Spirit, the Word that He decreed goes forth and produces what God the Father said.** So, it takes God the Father, the Word (the Lord Jesus) and the Holy Spirit for things to be created.

A lot of people read Genesis Chapter One and they immediately realize that they do not have to go far to find God the Father, God the Son, and God the Holy Spirit because they are all right there. **They can clearly see how it took the Holy Spirit to brood over the frozen deep, the Word of God to go forth by the power of the Holy Spirit and manifest what God the Father said.** This is why we Christians can boldly say that there are three persons in the Trinity or the Godhead and you can actually see them individually. You can see the Father, you can see the Lord Jesus Christ (the Word became flesh) and you can see the Lord Holy Spirit but they operate in unity and they function in unison. They are not divided because they are one.

Again, this is the point that the Apostle John was making to the Jewish people when he wrote the book of John. He told them that this very Jesus that you are looking at and that you are thinking has a devil because He said that He is **the I AM** is the very God that you read about in your Torah all the time. Even the Lord Jesus told them in **John 5:38-40** to go and search the scriptures because in them they think they will have life but that the scriptures are testifying of Him:

> "And ye have not his word abiding in you: for whom he hath sent, him ye believe not. *39* **Search the scriptures; for in them ye think ye have eternal life: and they are they which testify of me**. *40* And ye will not come to me, that ye might have life."

As you read **John 1:9-12**, you will see that the Apostle John wanted the Jews to know that the Lord Jesus was actually their **Creator**. They have been expecting His coming as their **Messiah** but when He came to them in the person of **Jesus the Christ**, they ignorantly rejected Him:

> "That was the true Light, which lighteth every man that cometh into the world. *10* **He was in the world, and the world was made by him, and the world knew him not**. *11* He came unto his own, and his own received him not. *12* But as many as received him, to them gave he power to become the sons of God, even to them that believe on his name…"

God does not create without His Word, so if you want to know the essence of who Jesus is, then take a look at Him at work in Genesis Chapter One as **God's WORD**! For example, if you hear my voice on anyone of my CDs talking, you will say that you are listening to me because I and my voice are one and the same. So, when you hear the Lord talking, who are you hearing? The Father! This is why in His efforts to reveal Himself to the Jews, the Lord looked at them and declared that He that has seen Him has seen the Father also.

The Jews Disrespected the Lord Jesus

The Lord knew that a lot of the Jews as well as their leaders did not have a clue as to whom they were dealing with as they were calling Him names. Many of them said that He was an imposter, a blasphemer, a Samaritan, and that He had a devil. In saying these things to Him as well as the way they treated Him, they highly disrespected Him when He was here on earth.

Sometimes, they wanted to stone Him, other times they spat on Him because they thought that He was making Himself equal to God. At times, He would say something to them and they would wonder what in the world He was talking about because of their legalistic mindsets. For instance, one day He said the following in **Matthew 11:28:**

> **"Come unto me, all ye that labour and are heavy laden, and I will give you rest."**

Again, you can imagine the Lord Jesus boldly telling the Jewish people that He has the ability to give them rest and to deliver them from their heavy burdens. No man has ever made this type of claim or spoke so boldly, but He could make such bold and seemingly audacious statements because He knew who He was — God in a human body! The Lord knew that the Jews were in the dark and that He is the light that came down to shine on them so that they can come out of the darkness that they were in, but they rejected Him. Also, because many of the leaders were not willing to accept Him and His ministry, they misled a lot of the Jewish citizens concerning His identity. Today, we are to learn from their mistakes and to take the Lord Jesus and His words very seriously.

Again, the Lord Jesus is the Word of God and He has always been with God the Father from the beginning but how did God get His Word into a human body? The next chapter will help us to further understand the power of the Word of God in a human body.

Chapter 8
How Jesus <u>Came Out</u> of GOD

Why God Sent His Word into a Human Body

God and His Word have always dwelt together in eternity and they had no need to be separated from each other until sin came into the world. **In order to deal with the problem of sin, God needed a man on earth that had no sin to help Him defeat sin in humanity.** Therefore, the Godhead (Trinity) made a decision to provide a human body for God's WORD to dwell in.

God the Father as the almighty God that can do anything spoke His Word into a human womb and that Word came out as a baby. This is why according to **Hebrews 10:5-9**, before the Lord Jesus came into the earth, He declared to God the Father in the realm of the Spirit thus:

> "Wherefore when he cometh into the world, he *(Jesus)* saith, Sacrifice and offering thou *(God the Father)* wouldest not, **but a body hast thou prepared me**: 6 In burnt offerings and sacrifices for sin thou hast had no pleasure. 7 **Then said I, Lo, <u>I come (in the volume of the book it is written of me,)</u>** *[meaning the written Word of God]* **to do thy will, O God.**
>
> 8 Above when he said, Sacrifice and offering and burnt offerings and offering for sin thou wouldest not, neither hadst pleasure therein; which are offered by the law; 9 **Then said he** *(Jesus)*, **Lo, <u>I come to do thy will</u>, O God...**"

From the above scripture, you can see that **the Lord Jesus is the embodiment of the Word that God the Father spoke, the Word of God that was written in the Torah and the Word of**

God that has been prophesied! <u>What God the Father did in His Son was prepare a human body to house His Word and for that body to walk about on earth a bona fide human being and a bona fide Son of God</u>! This was why the Lord declared in *verse 5* of the scripture above that *"a body hast thou prepared (for) me;"* confirming that yes, God prepared a human body for His Word (His Son) to dwell in on earth.

What this tells us is that the Word of God has power beyond our human imaginations. It is the reason that God wants us to live by it and to trust in it. It saves, delivers and heals; it is the powerful Word of the only Living and Sovereign God.

God's Word that a Virgin Shall Conceive

God had already given the Jewish people a prophecy (written Word) that a virgin shall conceive and bring forth a child and that the child will be **Emmanuel**; <u>meaning God with us</u> in **Isaiah 7:14:**

> "Therefore the Lord himself shall give you a
> sign; **Behold, a virgin shall conceive, and bear
> a son, and shall call his name Immanuel.**"

At the appointed time, God sent His WORD into the womb of a little 16 years old virgin named Mary with the announcement that she will conceive by the power of the Holy Spirit and bear a son (spoken Word). She was told to name the child **JESUS** because He will be the **Savior** — **Luke 1:30-37:**

> "And the angel said unto her, Fear not, Mary:
> for thou hast found favour with God. *31* **And,
> behold, <u>thou shalt conceive in thy womb,
> and bring forth a son, and shalt call his name
> JESUS</u>.** *32* **He shall be great, and shall be called
> the Son of the Highest: and the Lord God shall
> give unto him the throne of his father David:**

33 And he shall reign over the house of Jacob for ever; and of his kingdom there shall be no end *(this is the WORD of God that came to Mary).*

34 Then said Mary unto the angel, How shall this be, seeing I know not a man? 35 <u>And the</u> angel <u>answered and said unto her,</u> **The Holy Ghost shall come upon thee, and the power of the Highest shall overshadow thee:** <u>therefore</u> <u>also</u> <u>that holy thing which shall be born of thee</u> <u>shall be called the Son of God</u>... 37 **For with God nothing shall be impossible."**

True to His WORD, Mary was immediately pregnant with the Lord Jesus because she believed and received the WORD of God that was spoken to her through the Angel Gabriel. As a result, we can say that the Lord Jesus is the WORD of God **'tabernacled'** in a human body. It is an awesome display of God's power to do anything including giving His spoken WORD a human body. Can you image how the awesome WORD that came out of God the Father's mouth would go forth and become a human being? It is mind blowing when you really sit down to think about it.

Basically, the God wanted the Lord Jesus to be a sinless **'Adam'** (man) on earth for the plan of salvation that God has for humanity.

Jesus as the Second Adam
God created (the first) Adam by reaching down into dirt to pick up a lump of clay but with His well beloved Son; (the second Adam), it was enough that Mary His mother came out of clay. With the Lord Jesus, God did not have to reach into the dirt to produce Him. He said instead, "I am speaking this one into being."

Therefore, all Mary received was **an announcement of the WORD of God**. She received the WORD of God that said that

God has chosen her from among women and as a result, she will conceive and the holy child that she will bring forth will be of the Holy Ghost; meaning the Son of God. According to **Luke 1:38-44,** she received the announcement in faith:

> "**And Mary said, Behold the handmaid of the Lord; be it unto me according to thy word.** And the angel departed from her. *39* <u>And Mary arose in those days, and went into the hill country **with haste,** into a city of Juda;</u> *40* And entered into the house of Zacharias, and saluted Elisabeth.
>
> *41* <u>And it came to pass, that, when Elisabeth heard the salutation of Mary, the babe</u> *(John the Baptist)* <u>leaped in her womb; and Elisabeth was filled with the Holy Ghost:</u> *42* And she spake out with a loud voice, and said, Blessed art thou among women, and blessed is the fruit of thy womb.
>
> *43* **And whence is this to me, that the mother of my Lord should come to me**? *44* For, lo, as soon as the voice of thy salutation sounded in mine ears, the babe leaped in my womb for joy."

In the above scripture, Mary immediately went to visit her cousin Elisabeth who was already six months pregnant with John the Baptist. By the time Mary arrived at Elizabeth's house, she was also already pregnant with the Lord Jesus. The Word of God is powerful.

Jesus as God's Begotten Son

Because the Lord Jesus was spoken into being by His Father, we refer to Him as begotten. What this means is that He was not created but came out of God Himself. The Dictionary defines **'begotten'** as an *"offspring generated by procreation, of parents and children, related by blood, and biological child."* Therefore, as the only begotten of God the

Father, the Lord Jesus has God's natural DNA or blood! This is why He told us that He **proceedeth forth or came out from God** in **John 8:42:**

> "Jesus said unto them, If God were your Father, ye would love me: **for I** **proceeded** **forth and** **came from God**; neither came I of myself, but he sent me."

In other words, He was telling us that He came out of or began from God's mouth. The definition of **proceed** means: *To move, go forward or onward; to advance; to continue or renew motion begun; as to proceed on a journey.* As a result, we can now understand what the Lord was saying that He began or came forth from God the Father. **The humanity of Jesus (the Word of God) began the moment God's Word was spoken to Mary.** The Holy Spirit made the Word to become flesh (human) in Mary's womb. Therefore, it pays to know how God operates with His Word concerning humanity.

Why Can God Not Provide Himself a Son?

Some religions reject Jesus as God's Son because many of them do not know that God produced the Lord Jesus by His spoken WORD. As a result, you will meet people; especially those from the Islamic religion who think that it is the ultimate disrespect and the height of blasphemy to say that God has a Son. They actually get offended when they hear a Christian say that the Lord Jesus is **the Son of God** or that God has a Son. They are willing to believe that the Lord Jesus is the son of Mary and a Prophet but they will not accept Him as the Son of God. As a result, they ignorantly denounce the Lord Jesus as God's Son.

It is the reason why the Koran decries the Christian belief that Jesus is the **Son of God** in Sura 6:100 verses 100 and 101 and again in Sura 72:3. For example, according to eye witness reports, there are prominent displays of abominable mosaic declarations denouncing that Jesus is **the Son of God** on the walls of the mosque in Jerusalem known as the Dome of the Rock. Below is such an abominable declaration:

> "O People of the Book! Do not exaggerate in your religion nor utter aught concerning God save the truth. The Messiah, Jesus son of Mary, was only a Messenger of God, and His Word which He conveyed unto Mary, and a spirit from Him. So believe in God and His messengers, and say not 'Three' —Cease! (it is) better for you! —God is only One God. **Far be it removed from His transcendent majesty that He should have a son.**" and "**God, Who hath not taken unto Himself a son.**"

One of the reasons why they can parade this type of ignorance is because they think that in order for God to have a Son, He would have to sleep with or make love to a woman. What they do not understand is that when God made the first Adam, He did not need another person; all He needed was some dirt (a lump of clay). Every human being is a decedent of the first Adam. **To create Adam, God did not sleep with any woman to start the human family. Therefore, He did not need to sleep with a woman to provide Himself a Son.**

If they are willing to see the truth, they will ask themselves the following question: Why can God not provide Himself a Son when He needed a Son to save humanity? **If God was not able to provide Himself a Son, then, He would be limited in His abilities and any entity with limited abilities is no God but we know that the Judeo-Christian God can do all things. He is not limited in anyway, shape or form.**

Those who lean to their own understanding get blinded in their knowledge of God and as a result, they reject Him when He comes to them in a way that they have not known. Also, you can see that the Muslims have ignorantly rejected the Godhead or the Trinity because they have no knowledge of who God really is. They were sold a very big lie about the Lord Jesus and many of them still choose to believe that lie instead of the truth that is in the Bible.

Another thing is that Christianity predates Islam. Mohammed was not even born until 500 years after the death and resurrection of the Lord Jesus. Therefore, their attempt to rewrite the human history and in particular Christianity is nothing but a woeful failure for all to see except those who are blinded by their lies.

My Encounter with Some Muslim Women and Their Belief about Jesus

Some years ago, I met with a group of Muslim women and I sat down with them and after several minutes of my interaction with them, I began to share with them about the Lord Jesus. They were quick to inform me that they believe that He was the son of Mary and that He was a Prophet but when it comes to Him being the Son of God, they said it was impossible and blasphemous. **I asked them to tell me who a Muslim barren man or woman would cry out to when he or she needs a child and they told me God. Then I ask them how it is possible for God to give another person a child and yet is unable to provide Himself with one?**

I told them that God would not be God if He can give people what they want and yet cannot provide for Himself a Son to save humanity when He needed one. I asked them to think about it; how is it that God can give people children and cannot give Himself one? **I then began to explain to them where their reasoning went wrong. I told them that it was because they think that God will have to sleep or make love to a woman the way that men do on earth in order to produce a Son.**

I also told them that to begin the human family that we are all part of; God did not need a woman.

Therefore, when it came to providing Himself with a Son, all He had to do was send His Word into the womb of a woman without even leaving heaven and or getting up from His throne and 9 months later, the **Word** *came out as a child. They were stunned and speechless as they looked at me.*

As a Christian, you should be able to educate people from other religions about what makes Jesus different from Mohammed, Buddha, Krishna, Confucius, etc. <u>The truth is that all other men were created beings but the Lord Jesus was not created; he came forth from God Himself</u>! He is the spoken WORD of God that became flesh. In other words, the minute God spoke His first Words, there was Jesus!

Today, the Lord Jesus sits in heaven as a bona fide human being (without any blood flowing through His veins because He shed it all for our sins) and yet, He is a part of the Godhead. Those who are not Christians cannot even begin to understand the mystery of the Godhead or the Trinity and some of them who try, end up leading themselves and those who listen to them astray.

One of the things that I pointed out in the first of the three books in this series titled, ***Experiencing the Depths of God the Father*** is <u>how God wants to be known forever by all people</u>. Below is an excerpt on *pages 31-32:*

"And God said moreover unto Moses, **Thus shalt thou say unto the children of Israel, The <u>LORD God</u> of your fathers, <u>the God of Abraham</u>, <u>the God of Isaac</u>, and <u>the God of Jacob</u>, hath sent me unto you: <u>this is my name for ever</u>, and <u>this is my memorial unto all generations</u>.** *"*

Why would God say this about how He wants to be known forever as a perpetual memorial? God being ***All-Knowing*** *already foresaw that there would be a group of people today; billions of them as a matter of fact, who will* *be worshipping the God of Abraham and the God of Ishmael through the Islamic religion. Therefore, He tells us through Moses how He wants to be known and remembered forever — the God of Abraham, the God of Isaac and the God of Jacob.*

Although Ishmael and Isaac were both the sons of Abraham, God sovereignly chose to place the blessings of salvation and the right of inheritance in Isaac and not Ishmael because Isaac was the legitimate son by Abraham's wife while Ishmael was the son of a bond woman (a slave) — great difference between the children. Therefore, the Judeo God of Abraham, Isaac and Jacob that we worship in Christendom today is not the same God that the Ishmaelites are worshipping through the Islamic religion.

Again, they are worshipping the God of Abraham and Ishmael but we must always remember that the blessing is in Isaac and not in Ishmael. Moreover, God personally told us in the scriptures above how He wants to be known and remembered forever as a perpetual memorial of Him. Therefore, you must know Him and worship Him accordingly. When you come to God, you must know Him as the God of Abraham, the God of Isaac, and the God of Jacob so that you can receive the covenant blessings that He placed in Isaac through Abraham."

The whole reason for God doing this is to save fallen humanity and not so that people can have fancy religions with no provision for salvation. Therefore, come out of religion and let Christ give you eternal life. This life will enable you to live with God as His child forever; failure to do this means that you will not be able to live with God in all of eternity.

God Has Always Wanted to Have Children

From biblical accounts, angels worship God on a daily basis; the duty of some angels is to say, "Thou art holy" and

"Holy is the LORD" all day and every day. Although they are with God every day, they do not have a father-son or father-daughter relationship with Him. God yearned for children on earth and for a relationship with them. Therefore, God chose to bring many sons to Himself through the Lord Jesus' death and resurrection as we see in **Hebrews 2:9-11:**

> "But we see Jesus, who was made a little lower than the angels for the suffering of death, crowned with glory and honour; **that he by the grace of God should taste death for every man.** *10* **For it became him, for whom are all things, and by whom are all things, in** <u>**bringing many sons unto glory,**</u> **to make the captain of their salvation perfect through sufferings.** *11* <u>For both he that sanctifieth and they who are sanctified are all of one</u>: for which cause he is not ashamed to call them brethren."

The Lord is the first <u>begotten from the dead</u> as scriptures reveal in **Acts 26:23** because in Christ Jesus, God is raising up many sons and daughters. It was part of His salvation plan for man:

> "**That Christ should suffer, and that** <u>**he should be the first that should rise from the dead**</u>, and should shew light unto the people, and to the Gentiles."

It is again repeated in **Revelation 1:5:**

> "And from Jesus Christ, who is the faithful witness, **and the first begotten of the dead, and the prince of the kings of the earth.** Unto him that loved us, and washed us from our sins in his own blood…"

Why Jesus Had to Come to Earth

Why was it necessary for God to bring Jesus into the

earth? The answer is firstly, because God has always desired to dwell with humanity and for His children to rule and reign with Him on earth. Therefore, from Himself, He reproduced Himself in Christ with His spoken WORD. Secondly, because the first man that God created from clay (Adam) gave the title deed to the whole world (kingdom) away to the devil. As a result, the devil used this **"Adamic Authority"** to enslave all humanity without any human being able to escape from him.

For example, with this **'Adamic Authority'**, the devil could bring sickness, disease, destruction, hardship, misery and death upon any person that he wanted to. There was no one on earth that could withstand the devil. This is why the Lord Jesus had to come into the earth to bring us back to God and to deliver us from the devil's enslavement as stated in **Hebrews 2:14-17:**

> "Forasmuch then as the children are partakers of flesh and blood, he also himself likewise took part of the same; **that through death he might destroy him that had the power of death, that is, the devil; 15 And deliver them who through fear of death were all their lifetime subject to bondage.**
>
> 16 For verily he took not on him the nature of angels; **but he took on him the seed of Abraham. 17 Wherefore in all things it behoved him to be made like unto his brethren…"**

God looked at His creation and He was displeased at the misery that the devil was unleashing against humanity. Therefore, He decided to save His people from this enslavement by taking on a human form in the person of His Son Jesus. **The reason God needed a human being to take the kingdom or the title deed to the earth away from the devil was because God gave the earth to man and it**

was a man that lost it. Therefore, <u>it will have to take a man to regain or retake it from the devil</u>; this way, the earth will still remain in the hands of the children of men!:

> "The heaven, even the heavens, are the LORD'S **but the earth hath he given to the children of men**" (Psalm 115:16).

This is why you see that angels cannot preach the Gospel on earth because they do not have the **Adamic authority** that human beings have on earth. **Man is the only being God gave authority and dominion over the earth. As a result, only a man (Adam) can make decrees on earth. We are higher in God's hierarchy of creation than angels.** For example, when you are interceding or praying for a person to be saved, what an angel does is help steer the person's steps to be in the right place at the right time to meet you but <u>you</u> will have to speak the message of salvation to the person because angels do not have the Adamic authority on earth to speak as we have.

God's Plan to Redeem Man from the Devil's Enslavement

God wanted man redeemed from the devil and so, the Godhead came together in counsel and decided that the Son was going to come forth as a baby in Mary's womb and that He was going to be the **'Redemptive Lamb.'** As God's chosen lamb, He would undertake and accomplish everything that needed to be done in order to buy man back from sin. At this point, the devil had led all humanity into sin and into rebellion against God. Therefore, every human being was under God's judgment that the soul that sins must die as stated in **Ezekiel 18:4:**

> "**Behold, all souls are mine;** as the soul of the father, so also the soul of the son is mine: **the soul that sinneth, it shall die.**"

Also, God said that any man that sheds another man's blood, his blood must be shed and that an eye will be demanded from anyone that causes another to lose his or her eye. This is why the LAW is called "an eye for an eye":

> "And if any mischief follow, then thou shalt give life for life, 24 **Eye for eye, tooth for tooth, hand for hand, foot for foot,** 25 **Burning for burning, wound for wound, stripe for stripe"** (Exodus 21:23-25).

As we learned in scriptures, no man could keep the righteous requirements of the Law. Eventually, God had to send His Son to come down from heaven to fulfill the righteous requirements of the Law and to save us. The LAW required that every year, the children of Israel observe the Passover and kill bulls and goats in order for God to cover their sins. Because the blood of bulls and goats are not powerful enough to remove sin; every year, they had to kill another bull or another goat in order to cover their sin for another year. **In Christ Jesus, God wanted to deal with the problem of sin once and for all.**

His highest desire was not all those bloody bulls and goats that were being slaughtered. What God wanted was a perfect sacrifice that will take care of the problem of sin for all time. This is why the Lord Jesus said, **"but a body hast thou prepared me... I come to do thy will, O God."** He knew why He was coming into the earth and **He knew that His body was prepared specially to be sacrificed.** Yes, He knew that He was the perfect sacrifice for sin. His words in **Hebrews 10:5-9** that we read before are repeated and elaborated upon in **Psalm 40:6-9** below:

> **"Sacrifice and offering thou didst not desire; <u>mine ears hast thou opened</u>: burnt offering and sin offering hast thou not required. 7 Then said I, Lo, I come: in the volume of the book it is written of me, 8 <u>I delight to do thy will, O my God</u>: <u>yea, thy law is within my heart.</u> 9 I have preached righteousness in the great**

**congregation: lo, I have not refrained my lips,
O LORD, thou knowest."**

The Lord Jesus came into the earth to do His Father's will which was to go to the Cross as a lamb and die to pay for the sin of sinful humanity.

The Problem of Sin

When Adam and Eve sinned against God, God would have immediately dealt with the problem of sin had they repented of their sin before God. Even when God came on the scene and offered them an opportunity to repent, they did not. Instead, they went into the blame game. We can actually see for ourselves in **Genesis 3:8-13** exactly how they responded when God came on the scene:

> "And they *(Adam and Eve)* <u>heard the voice of the LORD God walking in the garden in the cool of the day</u>: and Adam and his wife hid themselves from the presence of the LORD God amongst the trees of the garden. 9 And the LORD God called unto Adam, and said unto him, Where art thou?
>
> 10 And he said, I heard thy voice in the garden, and I was afraid, because I was naked; and I hid myself. 11 *(God decided to give them the opportunity to repent)* And he said, Who told thee that thou wast naked? **Hast thou eaten of the tree, whereof I commanded thee that thou shouldest not eat?** *(Instead of repenting by saying I am sorry, Adam blamed Eve).*
>
> 12 <u>And the man said,</u> **The woman whom thou gavest to be with me,** <u>she gave me</u> **of the tree, and I did eat.** 13 And the LORD God said unto the woman, What is this that thou hast done? <u>And the woman said,</u> **The serpent <u>beguiled me</u>, and I did eat.**"

Because Adam and Eve did not repent, their sin remained and the Bible tells us that without repentance there is no remission of sin (Luke 13:3). Since we all descended from them, they passed their sin nature on to every human being on earth. **If you look at** *verse 8* **of the above scripture, you will notice that there was an immediate change in the relationahip between God and Adam and Eve. I always wondered Why God's <u>voice was walking in the garden</u>? Below is His explanation to me about it.**

According to Him, Adam and Eve had always beheld His glorious face from the day that they were created but the minute they sinned, they were immediately seperated from God and could now only hear the voice of the LORD God (the Word) walking in the garden. <u>Meaning that the Lord Jesus as the WORD immediately took on the role of Mediator or an Intermediary (the Lamb) between a Holy God and sinful man (Adam)</u>. Therefore, at the appointed time, the Lord Jesus came into the world to be God's perfect sacrifice for the sin of humanity. Again, He came as God's LAMB.

The truth of the matter is that the Lord Jesus as the LAMB of God **was slain the day that Adam and Eve sinned because God chose to have mercy on them before judging them**. Scriptures tells us that God killed a **Lamb** and that He used the skin and the blood of the **Lamb** to cover Adam and Eve in the garden before driving them out — **Genesis 3:21:**

> "Unto Adam also and to his wife did the **LORD God <u>make coats of skins</u>, and <u>clothed them</u>.**"

This is the beginning of the perfect sacrifice that God was going to manifest on earth. **Without this act of mercy by God, there would have been no redemptive provision for man.** I will discuss this fully in an upcoming Chapter titled, *Jesus as God's Chosen Lamb.*

When you read one of my books titled, ***How to Discern and Expel Evil Spirits,*** you will see how I outlined the reasons God revealed to me about why He chose to redeem us. You will also understand the reason that salvation is by His grace. For example, <u>when the 'non-human' people that lived on earth before Adam was created</u> (**"Pre-Adamic beings"**) <u>sinned against God, He judged them and stripped them of their terrestrial bodies</u> (bodies that can relate to material things on earth). According to Ezekiel 28, there were people that formed sanctuaries on earth that God gave Lucifer charge over. He was their praise and worship leader and they were the congregation that God referred to in Ezekiel 28 and that were corrupted by Lucifer. They joined with him in his rebellion against God. Lucifer was already abased by God to the status of a devil and a serpent before God created Adam. Therefore, the people in Ezekiel 28 are not the human beings of today but the devils or demons that are now contending with every human being.

<u>Not only did God create Adam as the replacement of both the **'Pre-Adamic beings'** and Lucifer with the ability to love and worship God, He did something that He had never done before with any other creation or work of His hands</u> — **He breathed His own breath into Adam!** He spoke all other creation into being but when it came to Adam; after He picked up the clay, He spat His own saliva into the clay because He never got water from anywhere else and He proceeded to mold the clay. After molding the clay, the Bible says He breathed into the clay (man) "and man became a living soul;" **meaning that man not only came alive but he became a part of God!**

This is why we are different from all of God's other creations including angels. This is also why God had mercy on Adam and Eve even after their blame game and without repenting. He showed them and their descendants (us) mercy because He had invested Himself in us. Again, He could show us mercy because of the part of Him that is in Adam.

You and I are sitting here today because of that breath which we call the Spirit from God. The day His breath departs from your body, you will see the body immediately begin to decompose and return back to the clay or the dust that it was before God's breath entered into it. **This is why when you look closely at the judgment that came upon Adam, you will see how God carefully made sure that the part of Him that was in Adam was not subjected to the judgment.** God's judgment on Adam is in **Genesis 3:17-19:**

> "And unto Adam he said, <u>Because thou hast hearkened unto the voice of thy wife, and hast eaten of the tree, of which I commanded thee, saying, Thou shalt not eat of it</u>: **cursed is the ground** for thy sake; <u>in sorrow shalt thou eat of it all the days of thy life;</u>
>
> 18 Thorns also and thistles shall it bring forth to thee; and thou shalt eat the herb of the field; 19 In the sweat of thy face shalt thou eat bread, **till thou return unto the ground; for out of it wast thou taken: for dust thou art, and unto dust shalt thou return."**

See how **God put the curse on the ground** because <u>Adam was of two parts</u>. **A part of Him is God's and the other part of him is from the earth. God breathed His own life into Adam so Adam carries the breath of God and as a result, if God puts the curse directly on Adam, God would be putting a curse on Himself as well.** In His wisdom, He put the curse on the ground so that the part of Adam that is from the ground would receive the curse and the part of Him that is from God would be safe. It is the reason why our spirits will never die but our bodies that are from the ground are subject to death.

God's commandment to Adam was, "<u>In the day that you eat of the fruit of that tree, you shall surely die</u>." Therefore, the judgment of death immediately came upon the part of

Adam that was from the earth but at the same time, God knew that He had to redeem Adam and his descendants by killing a lamb and covering him with its blood. As a result, He prepared **a body** to come into the world as a human being first; to manifest on earth the work God did in the Garden of Eden when he killed an innocent lamb and then, to effectively take on the devil and to set us free.

If Jesus had not come into the world, God would not have charged the devil with any crime because Adam gave the devil the authority to be Lord over the earth. Although the devil was not a righteous judge because he was misusing his authority over the earth, God could not bring charges against him. The reason for this was that all the people that the devil enslaved had also sinned against God; both the devil and man were rebels. According to God' righteous requirements, everyone that the devil enslaved deserved some form of death or another because we had sinned against God. God decided to bring a man into the world that would fulfill all His righteousness as a result qualify to judge all rebel on earth. At the same time, this same man will take on the devil and defeat him.

Chapter 9
Jesus as God's Chosen LAMB

In this chapter, we are going to see how God began the process of making Jesus His Chosen Lamb from the very beginning. It will help us to clarify our understanding of Jesus as the lamb of God.

God Began the 'Ransom Principle' in the Garden

Let us take a look at the way that God put into place this principle that we call the **'Ransom Principle'** or the **'Principle of Substitution.'** It is a principle that allows you to substitute an innocent person for a person who is guilty; in this case, the innocent Lord Jesus Christ for all of guilty humanity. As we saw in the last chapter, God began this principle in the Garden of Eden when He killed an innocent lamb and used its blood and skin to cover Adam and Eve's sin of rebellion against Him in **Genesis 3:7-21:**

"And the eyes of them both were opened, and they knew that they were naked; and they sewed fig leaves together, and made themselves aprons. 8 And they heard the voice of the LORD God walking in the garden in the cool of the day: and Adam and his wife hid themselves from the presence of the LORD God amongst the trees of the garden.

9 And the LORD God called unto Adam, and said unto him, Where art thou? 10 And he said, I heard thy voice in the garden, and I was afraid, because I was naked; and I hid myself. 11 And he said, Who told thee that thou wast naked? Hast thou eaten of the tree, whereof I commanded thee that thou shouldest not

eat?... 21 **Unto Adam also and to his wife did the LORD God make** <u>coats of</u> **skins** (*animal skins*)**, and clothed them."**

God Continued the 'Ransom Principle' in the Days of Moses

God continued this 'principle of substitution' or the 'ransom principle' in the days of Moses concerning the **Passover Lamb** while they were in Egypt. He later made it a law of atonement whereby an innocent goat (scapegoat) is held responsible for the sins of the people. You read about this in the Old Testament concerning the two goats that God required the children of Israel to present to the High Priest Aaron every year to make atonement for their sins. Aaron as the High Priest was to first examine the goats to make sure that they were fit for sacrifice or that they were without spot or blemish and he was to then cast lots between the two goats.

<u>The goat whose lot falls to the Lord will be sacrifice for sin offering</u> and the other goat will be designated as the 'scapegoat' to bear the sins of the people. This 'scapegoat' is therefore held responsible for all the sins of the people because Aaron is to confess the sins of the people upon this goat and then drive it into the wilderness to carry the sins of the people away: We see this recorded in **Leviticus 16:5-10:**

> **"And he shall take of the congregation of the children of Israel two** <u>**kids of the goats**</u> **for a sin offering... 8 And** <u>**Aaron shall cast lots upon the two goats**</u>**; one lot for the LORD, and the other lot for the scapegoat.** 9 <u>And Aaron shall bring the goat upon which the LORD'S lot fell, and offer him for a sin offering.</u> 10 **But the goat, on which the lot fell to be the** <u>scapegoat</u>**, shall be presented alive before the LORD, to make an atonement with him, and** <u>**to let him go for a scapegoat into the wilderness.**</u>**"**

When John the Baptist looked at the Lord Jesus, he knew by divine revelation that the Lord was the **'Perfect Lamb'** that had **no spot or blemish**. It was the reason why he asked the Lord, "Are you coming to me to baptize you? It is I who need You to baptize me." For a man of John the Baptist's caliber, it was a great honor to be the one to baptize God's Son:

> "Then cometh Jesus from Galilee to Jordan unto John, to be baptized of him. *14* **But John forbad him, saying, I have need to be baptized of thee, and comest thou to me?** *15* And Jesus answering said unto him, Suffer it to be so now: for thus it becometh us to fulfill all righteousness. Then he suffered him" (Matthew 3:13-15).

Jesus as the 'Scapegoat' or the Ransom Lamb

Again, the 'scapegoat' takes the blame for the sins of the entire nation. Therefore, as God's ransom (the innocent that takes the blame for the guilty); the Lord Jesus had to fulfill the requirements of both the goat killed for sin offering and the 'scapegoat'. Since the religious leaders of His day wanted nothing to do with Him, God needed someone on earth to declare the Lord Jesus as His chosen 'goat to be sacrificed for sin' (the goat that falls to the Lord when the lot is cast according to Leviticus 16:9). This is why it was necessary for John the Baptist; the son of a priest to examine the Lord Jesus and declare Him fit as the **Lamb** to be slaughtered for the sin of the world in **John 1:29-36:**

> "The next day John seeth Jesus coming unto him, and saith, **Behold the Lamb of God, which taketh away the sin of the world.** *30* **This is he of whom I said, After me cometh a man which is preferred before me: for he was before me.** *31* And I knew him not: but that he should be made manifest to Israel, therefore am I come baptizing with water. *32* And John bare record,

saying, I saw the Spirit descending from heaven like a dove, and it abode upon him.

33 And I knew him not: but he that sent me to baptize with water, the same said unto me, Upon whom thou shalt see the Spirit descending, and remaining on him, the same is he which baptizeth with the Holy Ghost. 34 And I saw, and bare record that this is the Son of God. 35 Again the next day after John stood, and two of his disciples; 36 And looking upon Jesus as he walked, **he saith, Behold the Lamb of God!"**

Also, since the High Priest on earth would not fulfill his duties concerning the Lord Jesus as the 'scapegoat', God who is higher than the High Priest had to personally declare Him fit at His baptism both as His Son and His Lamb as recorded in **Mark 1:9-11:**

"And it came to pass in those days, that Jesus came from Nazareth of Galilee, and was baptized of John in Jordan. 10 And straightway coming up out of the water, he saw the heavens opened, and the Spirit like a dove descending upon him: 11 And there came a voice from heaven, saying, **Thou art my beloved Son, in whom I am well pleased."**

Again, **Since the High Priest failed to fulfill his duty of releasing the 'scapegoat' (Jesus) into the wilderness, the Holy Spirit had to fulfill the duty that the High Priest would have fulfilled in confessing the sins of the people on the 'scapegoat' and then driving it into the wilderness.** This is why St. Mark tells us that the Holy Ghost drove the Lord into the wilderness right after His baptism and right after both God the Father and John the Baptist publicly declared His identity and qualification as the **Lamb of God** in **Mark 1:12-13.** In other words, God the Father approved of His Son as the **Lamb to be sacrificed** and God the Holy Spirit drove Him into the wilderness as the 'scapegoat'.

> **"And immediately the Spirit driveth him into the wilderness.** 13 And he was there in the wilderness forty days, tempted of Satan; and was with the wild beasts..."

Clearly, the Lord Jesus fulfilled both the requirements of the two goats: the one for sin offering and the one designated as the 'scapegoat'! It was necessary for the Holy Spirit to drive Him into the wilderness as the 'scapegoat' As the **Lamb of God**, He took on Himself the sin of the whole world.

The Use of the Blood of the Ransom

Leviticus 16:14-16 outlines how the children of Israel were to make atonement for their sins with the blood of bulls and goats. God's instructions were very specific:

> **"And he** *(Aaron)* **shall take of the blood of the bullock, and sprinkle it with his finger upon the mercy seat eastward; and before the mercy seat shall he sprinkle of the blood with his finger seven times.**
>
> 15 <u>**Then shall he kill the goat of the sin offering, that is for the people, and bring his blood within the vail, and do with that blood as he did with the blood of the bullock, and sprinkle it upon the mercy seat, and before the mercy seat:**</u>
>
> 16 **And he shall make an atonement for the holy place, because of the uncleanness of the children of Israel, and because of their transgressions in all their sins:** <u>and so shall</u>

<u>he</u> <u>do for the tabernacle of the congregation,</u> <u>that</u> <u>remaineth among them in the midst of</u> <u>their</u> <u>uncleanness."</u>

Remember that in the days of Moses, God would come and He would sit on the **Mercy Seat** between the two Cherubims in the Holy of Holies so, when the blood touches the **Mercy Seat**, it covers the sins of the people before God for that year so that their sins do not come into God's remembrance? Otherwise, God will have to judge their sins because **He is a very righteous God who will by no means acquit the guilty.** For example, the blood of the first man (Abel) that was killed on earth by Cain his brother is still crying out for vengeance to this day.

Abel's blood is crying out to God saying, "Avenge me, Oh God," and one of God's titles is **"the avenger of the oppressed or the powerless."** As a result, all vengeance belongs to Him and He springs into action to defend those who cry out to Him. Therefore, in order to hold God's hand from delivering judgment, the children of Israel always had to make blood sacrifices.

Even all the animal blood sacrifices were not enough because **Hebrews 10:1-4** below reveals that the blood of the animals that the children of Israel were sacrificing to cover their sins <u>could not forever remove their sins</u>. Therefore, every year, they had to kill new bulls, new lambs, and new goats:

> **"For the law having a shadow of good things to come, and not the very image of the things, <u>can never with those sacrifices which they offered year by year continually make the comers thereunto perfect.</u> 2 <u>For then would they not have ceased to be offered? because that the worshippers once purged should have had no more conscience of sins.</u> 3 <u>But**

<u>in those sacrifices there is a remembrance</u> <u>again made of sins every year</u>. **4 For it is not possible that the blood of bulls and of goats should take away sins."**

As we already saw in the scriptures, the children of Israel mastered the **'principle of substitution'** that required them to bring to God two goats. <u>The priest is to kill the first goat and its blood used to sanctify and sprinkle the Mercy Seat</u> as **"the blood of sprinkling."** With the second goat, he is to confess the sins of the people upon its head and release it into the wilderness bearing the sin of the entire nation as it goes in the wilderness to die there. Also, they were to sacrifice bulls and goats and to **sprinkle their blood upon the alter in order to sanctify the alter** in Leviticus 3:12-13:

> "And if his offering be a goat, then he shall offer it before the LORD. 13 **And he shall lay his hand upon the head of it, and kill it before the tabernacle of the congregation: and the sons of Aaron shall sprinkle the blood thereof upon the altar round about."**

Abraham and the Ransom Principle

When it came time for God to initiate the steps towards redeeming us from slavery to sin, He began a quest for a man on earth that He can use to carry out the plans in the earth realm. The process began in a very interesting way and we stand to learn some lessons from it because sometimes when God wants to bless you, He asks for the priciest thing you own or for that which you would be least willing to release to Him.

God came to Abraham and He took Abraham when he was about 70 years old from Babylon (Iraq) and sent him to Judea with a promise that his seed shall be numerous like the sand of the sea and the stars in the sky. Although God gave him this promise, yet he had no children by his wife Sarah and the two of them got very old. Finally, when he was 100 years old and his wife 90 years old, she had a baby boy after the Lord visited them and they named him Isaac — meaning laughter.

God knew that He would be giving to Abraham and to all humanity His very well beloved Son Jesus Christ. **Therefore, He set the stage for an exchange of sons to take place between Him and Abraham.** What am I talking about? I am talking about **"the principle of substitution or the ransom principle."** As I stated earlier, it is a principle in which the innocent is sacrificed for the sin of the guilty. To implement this principle of holding the innocent responsible for the sins of guilty humanity on earth, God needed Abraham's obedience.

After Isaac was born, Abraham and Sarah were very happy and they were grateful because God's Word that was spoken to them 25 years earlier; was now fulfilled and they have Isaac. Guess what; 12 or 13 years later, God demands that the child that they waited so long for, be sacrificed unto Him on Mount Moriah as recorded in **Genesis 22:1-10:**

> "And it came to pass after these things, that God did tempt Abraham, and said unto him, Abraham: and he said, Behold, here I am. 2 **And he said, Take now thy son, thine only son Isaac, whom thou lovest, and get thee into the land of Moriah; and offer him there for a burnt offering upon one of the mountains which I will tell thee of.**
>
> 3 And Abraham rose up early in the morning, and saddled his ass, and took two of his young men with him, and Isaac his son, and clave the wood for the burnt offering, and rose up, and

went unto the place of which God had told him. 4 Then on the third day Abraham lifted up his eyes, and saw the place afar off. 5 And Abraham said unto his young men, Abide ye here with the ass; and I and the lad will go yonder and worship, and come again to you.

6 And Abraham took the wood of the burnt offering, and laid it upon Isaac his son; and he took the fire in his hand, and a knife; and they went both of them together. 7 And Isaac spake unto Abraham his father, and said, My father: and he said, Here am I, my son. And he said, Behold the fire and the wood: but where is the lamb for a burnt offering?

8 And Abraham said, My son, <u>God will provide himself a lamb for a burnt offering</u> (*Abraham prophesied Jesus — God's lamb*): so they went both of them together. 9 And they came to the place which God had told him of; and Abraham built an altar there, and laid the wood in order, and bound Isaac his son, and laid him on the altar upon the wood. 10 **And Abraham stretched forth his hand, and took the knife to slay his son.**"

Think about this, He tells Abraham; take your son, <u>your only son whom you love</u> and go to Mount Moriah and sacrifice him to me! No one can imagine what initially went through the mind of Abraham when God requested that he kill the one child that he waited 25 years to have. Most of us cannot imagine God placing such a demand on us today. Really, how many people will be willing to give up their only child for God? The man Abraham was willing and in so doing, allowed God to activate the **'Ransom Principle'** through him.

We can safely say that the faith of Abraham came to the place where just like Job; he said, "Though he slays me yet will I serve him" **(Job 13:15)** and also like the Apostle Peter who said, "Where else shall we go, you have the words of eternal life" as recorded in **John 6:68**. You can also say that Abraham had counted the cost of following God and decided that if it costs him his Isaac, he was willing to go on with God. He was not willing to turn in another direction from God. He told himself that he had better obey God by sacrificing Isaac rather than run the risk of living without God in his life.

Therefore, he took Isaac and they went into the wilderness with his servants and he told the servant to wait while he and Isaac go to worship and that they will be back. He said this while knowing that he was going further away from them so that he can discretely sacrifice Isaac. The Bible says that he believed that even if he kills Isaac, God was able to raise Isaac back up from the dead. When they arrived in at the place of the sacrifice, Isaac who must have been young; about 12 or 13 years, asked his father where the lamb for the burnt offering was in **Genesis 22:7-8**:

> "And Isaac spake unto Abraham his father, and said, My father: and he said, Here am I, my son. **And he said, Behold the fire and the wood: but where is the lamb for a burnt offering?** *8* And Abraham said, My son, **God will provide himself a lamb for a burnt offering**: so they went both of them together."

It is important to note Abraham's response to Isaac that **"God will provide himself a lamb"** for a burnt offering. In so doing, Abraham prophesied that God was the one who will provide the lamb and as it turned out, God did and it was His Son Jesus. **This is the prophecy that placed a demand on God and made a way for Jesus to be born in the physical as the Lamb of God.** Remember that man

(Adam) is the one that God gave dominion over the earth? As a result, we are told in **Amos 3:7** that the Lord does nothing on earth unless He first reveals it to His servants the prophets. The reason is because God needs a man or a woman to release His Word into the earth realm so that it can be manifested. Whatever Adam (man) calls things (speaks) on earth so they are or so they become.

Since God involves man in His dealing on earth, Abraham prophesied that God was going to provide Himself a lamb and his decree on earth was honored by God. We see the Lord immediately responding in **Genesis 22:12-13 by truly giving Abraham a lamb.** He stopped Abraham from sacrificing his son Isaac when Abraham lifted up his knife to kill Isaac:

> "And he *(God)* said, <u>Lay not thine hand upon the lad, neither do thou anything unto him: for now I know that thou fearest God, seeing thou hast not withheld thy son, thine only son from me</u>. 13 **And Abraham lifted up his eyes, and looked, and behold behind him a ram caught in a thicket by** his horns: and Abraham went and <u>**took the ram, and offered him up for a burnt offering in the stead of his son**</u>."

At the end of their encounter, God gave Abraham a ram (lamb) to sacrifice in place of his son Isaac. Thus, the man Abraham released God's hand to move on behalf of humanity. This is the **'principle of substitution'** because the lamb replaced Isaac. In other words, instead of Abraham offering Isaac, God gave Abraham an innocent lamb; the innocent lamb took the place of the guilty Isaac (man).

The significance of the exchange between God and Abraham was that God was looking for someone who was willing to give God his best and Abraham showed God that he was willing to give Him his very best — Isaac! What it further means is that when God saw that Abraham was willing to give up his only beloved son Isaac, God also gave up His only begotten Son Jesus to become the **'scapegoat'** and the **Lamb** to be sacrificed for the sin of humanity — Hebrews 11:17:

> "**By faith Abraham, when he was tried, offered up Isaac: and <u>he that had received the promises</u>** *(God)* <u>**offered up his only begotten son**</u>."

What Abraham did opened the door for the sacrifice that God made thousands of years earlier in the Garden of Eden to be manifested in the earth realm. <u>The blood of God's lamb covered Adam and Eve in the realm of the spirit but it needed to be manifested in the physical realm.</u> Always remember that things happen first in the realm of the spirit before they are manifested in the earth. Therefore, Jesus as the **Lamb of God** was slain from the <u>foundation of the world</u>; meaning the day that man sinned and God immediately covered man with the blood and the skin of a lamb — Genesis!

Just as Abraham took his beloved Isaac to Mount Moriah to be sacrificed, God's only begotten Son (the Lord Jesus) that He gave for the sin of guilty humanity was also crucified on Golgotha better known as Calvary! Our God is a very faithful covenant keeper.

The Significance of the Blood of Jesus

The Lord Jesus was the Perfect Lamb to be sacrificed for sin and He was because all mankind sinned and all became guilty before God. There was no way that we could pay by ourselves for our <u>sin</u> in order to fulfill the righteous requirements of God. **Therefore, as the Lamb of God and after His resurrection, the Lord Jesus did in heaven what the High Priests do here on earth in the Holy of Holies.** <u>Remember that the High Priest is to take the blood of the</u>

goat designated for sin offering into the Holy of Holies and sprinkle the Mercy Seat with it?

Well, the Lord Jesus (a Perfect Lamb) took His own blood and went into the Holy of Holies in heaven and offered it to God for the atonement of the <u>sin</u> of the world. As recorded in **Hebrews 9:11-14**, only the blood of Jesus can fully make atonement for the **<u>sin</u>** of all mankind:

> <u>"But Christ being come an **high priest** of good things to come</u>, by a greater and more perfect tabernacle *(His body)*, not made with hands, that is to say, not of this building; 12 **Neither by the blood of goats and calves, but by his own blood he entered in once into the holy place, having obtained eternal redemption for us.**

> "13 **For if the blood of bulls and of goats, and the ashes of an heifer sprinkling the unclean, sanctifieth to the purifying of the flesh:** 14 <u>**How much more shall the blood of Christ, who through the eternal Spirit offered himself without spot to God, purge your conscience from dead works to serve the living God?**</u>"

This is why we can say that the Lord Jesus paid our sin debt in full and God the Father was pleased with the payment. **He accepted the blood of His Son as an eternal payment for the sin of the world.** For humanity, this is awesome and we all should be forever grateful.

Believers Put on the Blood and Skin of God's Chosen Lamb

As I have mentioned before, the Lord Jesus was slain in the realm of the spirit the day that Adam and Eve sinned and His skin and blood became Adam and Eve's covering. When you read **Galatians 3:27-29**, the Apostle Paul tells us that those of us that are baptized into Christ have put on Christ just as Adam and Eve did! It is the same principle:

> **"For as many of you as have been baptized into Christ have put on Christ.** 28 There is neither Jew nor Greek, there is neither bond nor free, there is neither male nor female: for ye are all one in Christ Jesus. 29 And if ye be Christ's, then are ye Abraham's seed, and heirs according to the promise."

When you are baptized into Christ, you actually put on Christ in the realm of the spirit. This is why when you see the **'New Creation'** (a born again Christian) in the realm of the spirit, it is the profile of the Lord Jesus that you see. In other words, when you first look at a born again Christian in the spiritual realm, you will think that you are looking at the Lord Jesus because the **'New Creation'** looks just like Him!

It is when you come close to the person that you realize that it is not the Lord Jesus that you are looking at. Meaning that, as the person comes closer to you, you will begin to notice that the person's face has details of who the person truly is. It is a most amazing sight because the **'New Creation'** carries himself, walks, and acts just like the Lord Jesus. The entire profile is that of the Lord Jesus; it has His stature.

Again, the differences between the Lord Himself and the **'New Creation'** become apparent when you look at the person very closely because it is then that you begin to notice the facial expressions, and other things that preserve the person's original identity. Yes, from what I have seen several times, you actually put on Jesus Christ as your spiritual covering when you are baptized into Him.

Chapter 10
Why Many Stumble at the Identity of Jesus

Key to Why Many Stumble at Jesus' Identity

Some of the reasons why so many people stumble at the identity of the Lord Jesus Christ are found in **1 Corinthians 1:18-25.** Many people want to approach the identity of the Lord with their human intellect or logic and they stumble each time. Some other people want to see signs and wonders before they believe but God requires **faith in His Word** for the revelation of His Son:

> "For the preaching of the cross is to them that perish foolishness; but unto us which are saved it is the power of God. *19* For it is written, **I will destroy the wisdom of the wise, and will bring to nothing the understanding of the prudent.**

> *20* **Where is the wise? where is the scribe? where is the disputer of this world? hath not God made foolish the wisdom of this world? *21* For after that in the wisdom of God the world by wisdom knew not God**, it pleased God by the foolishness of preaching to save them that believe.

> *22* **For the Jews require a sign**, and the **Greeks seek after wisdom: *23* But we preach Christ crucified, unto the Jews a stumblingblock, and unto the Greeks foolishness; *24* But unto them which are called, both Jews and Greeks, Christ the power of God, and the wisdom of God. *25* Because the foolishness of God is wiser than men; and the weakness of God is stronger than men."

As you have just read from the above scripture, it takes faith to know the true identity of the Lord Jesus. Those who approach His identity with worldly wisdom or human logic will stumble and many have been doing so for centuries now. We are to learn from their mistakes.

One of the things a lot of people do not know is that God does not usually communicate with the human mind but with our human spirit. Therefore, those who want the things of God to make sense to them through logic or earthly wisdom, find the things of God difficult to believe and as a result, they regard them as foolish or superstitious. The **carnal mind** (the un-renewed or un-regenerated mind by the Word of God) cannot receive the things of God. We are told in **Romans 8:5-8** that the **carnal mind** is actually an enemy to the things of God:

> "For they that are after the flesh do mind the things of the flesh; but they that are after the Spirit the things of the Spirit. *6* <u>For to be carnally minded is death; but to be spiritually minded is life and peace.</u> *7* **Because the carnal mind is enmity against God: for it is not subject to the law of God, neither indeed can be.** *8* **So then they that are in the flesh cannot please God.**"

Again, the human mind kicks against the things of God because they do not make sense to it. This is why the Apostle Paul wrote the following in **1 Corinthians 2:4-12:**

> "And my speech and my preaching was not with enticing words of **man's wisdom**, but in demonstration of the Spirit and of power: *5* <u>That your faith should not stand in the **wisdom of men**,</u> but in the power of God. *6* **Howbeit we speak wisdom among them that are perfect: yet not the wisdom of this world, nor of the**

princes of this world, that come to nought: *7* But we speak the **wisdom of God in a mystery,** even the **hidden wisdom,** which God ordained before the world unto our glory:

8 **Which none of the princes of this world knew: for had they known it, they would not have crucified the Lord of glory.** *9* But as it is written, Eye hath not seen, nor ear heard, neither have entered into the heart of man, **the things which God hath prepared for them that love him.** *10* **But God hath revealed them unto us by his Spirit: for the Spirit searcheth all things, yea, the deep things of God.**

11 For what man knoweth the things of a man, save the spirit of man which is in him? **even so the things of God knoweth no man, but the Spirit of God.** *12* **Now we have received, not the spirit of the world, but the spirit which is of God; that we might know the things that are freely given to us of God."**

God reveals secrets and mysteries about Himself, His Son and His Holy Spirit only to those that love Him by believing His Word. When you choose to live by His Word and walk with Him, He will then begin to educate you concerning His kingdom. Remember the Lord Jesus' caution to us "not to cast our pearls before swine?" Well, if you refuse to believe or live by His Word, you leave Him no reason to reveal His secrets to you. He too will not cast His pearls before swines; **Matthew 7:6:**

"Give not that which is holy unto the dogs, **neither cast ye your pearls before swine,** lest they trample them under their feet, and turn again and rend you."

Jesus as the Perfect Image and Likeness of God

In **Genesis 1:26,** the Godhead (Elohim or **God the Father, God the Son** and **God the Holy Spirit**) decided that they wanted to make man in their image and after their likeness and they wanted this man to have dominion over the whole earth:

> "And God said, **Let us make man in our image, after our likeness**: and **let them have dominion** over the fish of the sea, and over the fowl of the air, and over the cattle, and over all the earth, and over every creeping thing that creepeth upon the earth."

This knowledge is very critical in our walk with God because this is the specimen of the man or the woman that God set out to create. At the end (Judgment Day), God is looking for that person who does not just look like Him but acts like Him. Meaning, a man or a woman that has His character, likes what God likes, hates what God hates, and walks the way God wants him or her to walk which is by the Word of God.

God will allow those who are demonstrating or reflecting this very specimen that God set out to create in Christ Jesus to rule and reign for Him on earth in the next millennium. **Since God is going to hold us accountable for how we allowed His Word to conform us to the image of His Son, we owe it to ourselves to truly understand what His Son's image and likeness are.**

Image Defined

An **image** is defined as an **imitation, representation,** or **similitude** of any person, thing, or act. **In our case, image here means physically looking similar to God.** When you behold God the Father, you will be shocked at how He looks just like a human being that you have seen before. The reason is because all human beings are physically in His image. He made us to look like Him physically and it is amazing how we all have an aspect of His expression. Some people have His smile to the tee, while others have His cheekbones, His forehead, the twinkle in His eye and I have actually even seen people that looked <u>almost</u> completely like Him because we all have His physical expressions.

Likeness Defined

A **Likeness** is defined as **the state, quality, or fact of being like; resemblance. It means an <u>imitative appearance</u>; a <u>semblance</u>. It means to look like and to <u>act like</u>** (meaning to have the character of).

The Lord Jesus is the perfect <u>image</u> and <u>likeness</u> of God. Meaning that He did not just look like God as a man made in God's image, **He demonstrated the perfect <u>character or attributes</u> of God for all to see when He was here on earth. He still does the same today from heaven.**

Jesus Reveals Himself

The Pharisees, the scribes and the scholars of Jesus' day did not take the time to study the scriptures about Him and as a result, every time they came around, they had a negative attitude towards Him. They questioned His identity, and they challenged His authority to speak and minister the way that He did.

Whenever they questioned His authority, He would tell them that He had already told them that He and God the Father are one and that God the Father sent Him to them but that they did not believe Him. One day, He told them that He that has seen Him has seen the Father; still one of His disciples named Philip demanded that He show them the Father and then they will be satisfied. In reply, the Lord told Philip that every time Philip has been looking at Him, he has also been looking at the Father. As a matter of fact, He told them that it is the Father that dwells in Him that really does the works of miracles through Him in **John 14:7-10:**

> **"If ye had known me, ye should have known my Father also: and from henceforth ye know him, and have seen him.** *8* <u>Philip saith unto him, Lord, shew us the Father, and it sufficeth us</u>. *9* Jesus saith unto him, **Have I been so long time with you, and yet hast thou not known me, Philip? he that hath seen me hath seen the Father; and how sayest thou then, Shew us the Father?**
>
> *10* **Believest thou not that I am in the Father, and the Father in me? the words that I speak unto you I speak not of myself: but the Father that dwelleth in me, he doeth the works."**

Finally, He told them that even if they do not believe that He is who He says He is; they should at least believe Him for the very works sake — **John 14:11:**

> "Believe me that I am in the Father, and the Father in me: **or else believe me for the very works' sake."**

One of the notable miracles of the Lord Jesus was His healing of a man that was born blind and who was over 40 years old. In **John 9:24-34,** even the previously blind man told the Jewish leaders that it had never been known that somebody born blind and over 40 years, could regain his sight the way he did through a miracle performed by the Lord Jesus Christ. He concluded that no one can do such a miracle unless God was with the person because giving sight back to someone that has been blind for over 40 years has to be an act of God, but still, they did not want to hear it. Instead, they began to reproach the previously blind man and they tossed him out of their midst:

> "Then again called they *(the leaders)* the man that was blind, and said unto him, Give God the praise: we know that this man is a sinner. 25 **He answered and said, Whether he be a sinner or no, I know not: one thing I know, that, whereas I was blind, now I see.** 26 Then said they to him again, What did he to thee? how opened he thine eyes?
>
> 27 He answered them, I have told you already, and ye did not hear: wherefore would ye hear it again? will ye also be his disciples? 28 Then they reviled him, and said, Thou art his disciple; but we are Moses' disciples. 29 We know that God spake unto Moses: as for this fellow, we know not from whence he is.
>
> 30 The man answered and said unto them, **Why herein is a marvellous thing, that ye know not from whence he is, and yet he hath opened mine eyes. 31 Now we know that God heareth not sinners: but if any man be a worshipper of God, and doeth his will, him he heareth.**
>
> 32 **Since the world began was it not heard that any man opened the eyes of one that was born blind. 33 If this man were not of God, he could do nothing.** 34 They answered and said unto him, Thou wast altogether born in sins, and dost thou teach us? And they cast him out.

One thing that we have to remember about the Lord Jesus is that; He is the same yesterday, today and forever (**Hebrews**

13:8). What He did while He was here on earth, He is still doing today from heaven. He still heals, delivers, and cast out devils **through His Church** that represent Him here on earth **as His body**.

Chapter 11
Jesus as the Heir of God

Definition of an Heir
An **heir** is someone **who stands to inherit all that the parent** owns or a person **who is entitled by law or by the terms of a will to inherit the estate of another.** It also means a person **who succeeds or is in line to succeed to a hereditary rank, title, or office.**

God Made Man His Earthly Heir in the Garden of Eden
When God created Adam (man) and placed him in the Garden of Eden, He gave Adam the title deed to the whole earth and He placed everything on earth under Adam's feet as we read in **Genesis 1:26-28:**

> "...**And let them have dominion over the fish of the sea, and over the fowl of the air, and over the cattle, and over all the earth, and over every creeping thing that creepeth upon the earth...** 28 And God blessed them, and God said unto them, <u>Be fruitful, and multiply, and replenish the earth, and subdue it</u>: **and have dominion over the fish of the sea, and over the fowl of the air, and** <u>over every living thing that moveth upon the earth.</u>"

We know that Adam gave away the title deed to the devil in no time at all but God in His wisdom had already made plans that His Son would come into the earth as a man and reclaim the title deed that Adam lost. Therefore, the Lord Jesus came into the earth as an "Adam" *(man)* to whom God bequeathed everything in heaven and on earth! Let us look at this aspect of the Lord Jesus.

Jesus is the True Heir of God

The original dominion over the earth as we already saw was given to Adam. As God's heir on earth, God placed His works in Adams hands. The Psalmist noted this in **Psalm 8:3-8:**

> **"When I consider thy heavens, the work of thy fingers, the moon and the stars, which thou hast ordained;** 4 What is man, that thou art mindful of him? and the son of man, that thou visitest him? 5 For thou hast made him a little lower than the angels, and hast crowned him with glory and honour.
>
> 6 **Thou madest him to have dominion over the works of thy hands; thou hast put all things under his feet:** 7 **All sheep and oxen, yea, and the beasts of the field;** 8 **The fowl of the air, and the fish of the sea, and whatsoever passeth through the paths of the seas."**

The first man (Adam) was given dominion over the whole earth but he lost that dominion to the devil. This is why when the devil encountered the Lord Jesus, he proudly showed the Lord the kingdoms of this world and their glory while announcing that **they were given to him** in **Luke 4:5-8:**

> "And the devil, taking him up into an high mountain, shewed unto him all the kingdoms of the world in a moment of time. 6 **And the devil said unto him, All this power will I give thee, and the glory of them: for that is delivered unto me; and to whomsoever I will I give it.**
>
> 7 If thou therefore wilt worship me, all shall be thine. 8 And Jesus answered and said unto him, Get thee behind me, Satan: for it is written, Thou shalt worship the Lord thy God, and him only shalt thou serve."

Now, you can now see why the Lord had to go head-to-head with the devil on the Cross and in hell so that He can take back the dominion that the devil swindled away from Adam in the Garden of Eden. **The Lord accomplished this task and as a result, He is the one that now exercises full dominion over the earth.** This is also stated in **Hebrews 2:5-10:**

> **"For unto the angels hath he not put in subjection the world to come, whereof we speak.** 6 But one in a certain place testified, saying, <u>What is man, that thou art mindful of</u> him? <u>or the son of man, that thou visitest him</u>? 7 <u>Thou madest him a little lower than the angels; thou crownedst him with glory and honour,</u> **and didst set him over the works of thy hands:**
>
> 8 **Thou hast put all things in subjection under his feet. For in that he put all in subjection under him, he left nothing that is not put under him.** <u>But now we see not yet all things put under him</u> *(meaning that not all men are walking in dominion yet).* 9 **But we see Jesus, who was made a little lower than the angels for the suffering of death, crowned with glory and honour; that he by the grace of God should taste death for every man.**
>
> 10 For it became him, for whom are all things, and by whom are all things, in bringing many sons unto glory, to make the captain of their salvation perfect through sufferings.

We need to always remember that God made Christ the heir of all that He has. What this means is that the Lord Jesus as God's only begotten Son has been given both ownership and charge over all of God's vast estates in heaven, earth and even hell!

We Are Now Heirs of God and Joint-heirs With Christ

The Lord Jesus is the only one that is currently walking in full dominion and He delegated this dominion power and authority to us who believe in Him before He left the earth. Also, the finished works of Christ allowed God the Father to make us (believers) His heirs and joint-heirs with Christ. In order for us to partake of this dominion power and authority that we inherited in Christ, God takes hold of us and He shakes the foolishness and ignorance out of us through tests and trials in order to re-orient us about Himself, His Son, His Spirit, and His kingdom.

While at it, He gives us a balanced view about money, people, prestige, reputation, material possessions, jobs, relationships, etc. As we grow in the character of His Son (the true Heir), He begins to allow us to also enjoy our new status of being heirs of God and joint-heirs with Christ. This means that we can begin to reign on earth for Him as it is written in **Romans 5:17** that:

> "...much more <u>they which receive abundance of grace and of the gift of righteousness</u> **shall reign in life by one, Jesus Christ.**"

God destined us in Christ to co-reign and rule with Him. Why? Because we have become bone of Jesus' bone and flesh of His flesh; we have put on Christ. We are truly heirs of God and joint-heirs with Christ!

Chapter 12
Jesus as the Sin of the World

In this Chapter, we are going to look at how the Lord Jesus took on not only the sin of the world, **but also, how He actually became the sin of the world in order to defeat <u>sin</u> for us.** First, let us get an understanding of what the sin of the world is.

What is the Sin of the World?

We need to know this in order to appreciate the fact that the Lord Jesus took it away. Remember that when John the Baptist saw the Lord Jesus, he referred to Him as the **Lamb of God** that takes away the <u>sin</u> of the world in **John 1:29?:**

> "The next day John seeth Jesus coming unto him, and saith, **Behold the Lamb of God, which taketh away the <u>sin</u> of the world.**"

According to scriptures, **there is only one <u>sin</u> of the world.** So, what is the <u>sin</u> of the world? **The sin of the world is <u>rebellion against God or disobedience to God's WORD!</u>** God and His Word are one. **Therefore, everything that we see that is wrong with the earth and the people in it today is the result of man's rebellion against God's Word in the Garden of Eden.** When you look at the nations or you hear of wars, murders, terrorism, organized crimes, gang wars, stealing, kidnappings, various sexual perversions, and all other acts of man's inhumanity to man, what you are seeing is the result of the increase of rebellion against God and His Word by man.

Just like blessings, <u>sin</u> has the propensity or ability to increase and with each generation on earth, <u>sin</u> is like hell; it enlarges itself as people find more and more ways to turn their backs on God and on His Word. As a result, <u>sin</u> is the major problem that God has had to deal with ever since the devil introduced it to God's perfect creation.

First, the devil taught rebellion against God to the Pre-Adamic beings that lived on earth before Adam was created (the beings that are now the demons that we contend with), then he taught rebellion to a third of God's angels in heaven and finally, he taught Adam and Eve rebellion against God. **Therefore, the Lord Jesus was God's solution to the problem of rebellion that He has with man.**

Also, the Lord Jesus is the only person that has lived on God's earth throughout His life time and did not sin against Him by rebelling against Him or His Word. Therefore, He was qualified to become the 'scapegoat' as we already saw in a previous chapter to take upon Himself the **sin** of the world — **2 Corinthians 5:21:**

> "**For he** (*meaning God*) **hath <u>made him</u>** (*Jesus*) **<u>to be sin for us</u>, who knew no sin;** that we might be made the righteousness of God in him."

The Lord Jesus literally became **a curse** before God as He hung on the Cross as the **sin of the world**. We see this recorded in **Galatians 3:13-14:**

> "<u>Christ hath redeemed us from the curse of the law</u>, **being made a curse for us:** <u>for it is written,</u> **Cursed is every one that hangeth on a tree** (*the Cross*): 14 That the blessing of Abraham might come on the Gentiles through Jesus Christ; that we might receive the promise of the Spirit through faith."

He had not only become our sin, he also became accursed in the sight of God as He hung on the Cross receiving in Himself, the punishment for all our sins.

Seeing Jesus on the Pole as 'the Sin of the World' in the Wilderness

We can also see the works that the Lord Jesus would do on the Cross displayed in the wilderness during the time of Moses in **Numbers 21:5-9.** When the children of Israel sinned against God and fiery serpents began to bite many of them in the camp, they cried to the Lord because many people died.

As a cure to the bites of the fiery serpents, God told Moses to place a fiery serpent (a symbol of sin) on a pole and to mount the pole up in the camp (a type of the Cross) and that it shall come to pass that whosoever looks upon the fiery serpent (the sin) on the pole after the person is bitten, that person shall live. **This single act of God through Moses was a demonstration of how the Lord Jesus was going to become our <u>sin</u> on the Cross** (the serpent on the pole):

> "And the people spake against God, and against Moses, Wherefore have ye brought us up out of Egypt to die in the wilderness? for there is no bread, neither is there any water; and our soul loatheth this light bread. 6 And the LORD sent fiery serpents among the people, and they bit the people; and much people of Israel died.
>
> 7 Therefore the people came to Moses, and said, We have sinned, for we have spoken against the LORD, and against thee; pray unto the LORD, that he take away the serpents from us. And Moses prayed for the people. 8 <u>And the LORD said unto Moses</u>, **Make thee a fiery serpent, and set it upon a pole: and <u>it shall come to pass, that every one that is bitten, when he looketh upon it, shall live</u>**.
>
> 9 And Moses made a serpent of brass, and put it upon a pole, **and it came to pass, that if a**

serpent had bitten any man, <u>when he beheld the serpent of brass, he lived.</u>"

Today, because the Lord Jesus has gone to the Cross for us, whoever looks up to Him (the serpent on the pole) is saved from their sins and trespasses against God. Knowing that He was going to the Cross to be hung, Jesus said the following that confirmed that He was going to become the 'sin of the world' in order to save humanity in **John 12:32:**

"And I, **if I be lifted up** from the earth, will draw all men unto me."

Jesus Learned Obedience

Before the Lord could go to the Cross as the **'sin of the world'** or become the **'scapegoat'** to be held responsible for the **sin of the world**, He too had to learn obedience as stated in **Hebrews 5:7-9**. Remember that He existed as God's Word in eternity but once He took on the nature of man, He had to learn and demonstrate His obedience to God the Father:

"**Who** *(Jesus)* <u>in the days of his flesh, when he had offered up prayers and supplications with strong crying and tears unto him that was able to save him from death, and was heard in that he feared;</u> 8 **Though he were a Son, yet learned he obedience by the things which he suffered;**

9 **And being made perfect, he became the author of eternal salvation unto all them that obey him.**"

This is why when you come into the kingdom today, the lesson of obedience is your number one lesson from the Lord. When we come to God, He gives us the gift of righteousness in Christ but He surely sees to it that we all learn obedience; even if it means great suffering for us. Therefore, it does not matter how rich you are, it does not matter what type of reputation you have, it does not matter what you think of yourself or how you have propped yourself up, **God must teach you that man shall not live by bread alone <u>but by every WORD that proceedeth out His mouth</u>:**

> "And he humbled thee, and suffered thee to hunger, and fed thee with manna, which thou knewest not, neither did thy fathers know; **that he might make thee know that man doth not live by bread only, but by every word that proceedeth out of the mouth of the LORD doth man live**" (Deuteronomy 8:3).

If you are stubborn, He will take you through the land flowing with scorpions, serpents (wicked spirits) and all kinds of wicked people to get you to learn the lesson of obedience according to **Deuteronomy 8:15**:

> **"Who led thee through that great and terrible wilderness, wherein were fiery serpents, and scorpions, and drought, where there was no water;** who brought thee forth water out of the rock of flint."

If it takes you 50 years to learn it, He is willing to go the long haul. Why? Because, He would rather have you spend 50 years in misery learning obedience than for you to spend eternity in hell. For example, a person can spend his or her life living in luxury on earth but in disobedience to God and His Word and at the end of the person's life, God has no choice but to reject the person.

Here is my account of how He dealt with me when I came to Him. I met the Lord in my early years when He raised me up again from the dead but as I grew, just like the children of Israel in the wilderness, the memory of what He did for me became dull and because I had professors in graduate school that were atheists, I gradually slipped into agnosticism (not sure if God exists or not). Once I got to this state of mind, it became difficult for me to listen to anyone who wants to talk to me about God or about religion; I had become stubborn. I also became enraged against God (if he existed) for His seemingly lack of love or care for black people. As a result, I viewed Christianity as an attempt to re-enslave black people and I wanted no part of it.

I became cured of my agnosticism in the psychiatric hospital 7 months after I became born again. In order to deal with my stubbornness towards Him, God allowed the devil 'to have a go at me' for a season. O, I became quickly convinced that not only does God exists, the devil and his demons also exist as well. They terrorized and tormented me for months. God took a drastic measure with me but He saw to it that I became aware of His existence and the existence of the devil. He made sure that I was cured of all agnosticism! I had to let go of the carnal mind once I started to study the Word of God.

The Fallen Man and the Word of God

As God showed in scriptures, man's 'fallen nature' is not subject to the Word of God; it is rebellious towards God. To prove this point, you will notice that as a child is growing up, you never have to teach the child how to lie or become selfish because it will come naturally to him or her. It starts when the child learns that his or her unrighteous actions have negative consequences. On the other hand, you have to spend a great deal of time trying to get the child to learn to tell the truth or to become obedient to his or her parents and to the laws of the land. This is why the Bible says in **Psalm 58:3** that:

> "The wicked are estranged from the womb: **they go astray as soon as they be born, speaking lies.**"

The 'fallen man's nature' does not like being told what to do. For example, when you try to share the Gospel of the kingdom or the Word of salvation with some people, their response is that you are trying to shove your religion down their throats, or that you are trying to impose your views upon them and they rebel against what you are saying to them. Little do they know that they are actually kicking against the Word of God in their rebellion.

I remember when I first became born again and I started spending a great deal of time in the Bible and praying. One of my relatives complained to my mother that I was reading the Bible and praying too much. The relative said to my mother, *"What sin has she committed that she stays up all night praying. Is she the one that killed Jesus Christ?"* On my part, I realized that I was the first person in my family to be guilty of this same offence because when I was not yet born again, I locked away my youngest sister's Bible. I thought that she read the Bible too much so I took away her Bible. In my opinion then, I thought that as an attorney, she was wasting time reading the Bible instead of using the time to actively practice her profession in the court of law.

The reason for these types of behaviors is because the things of God do not appeal to unbelievers. This is why after you give your life to the Lord and you become serious in your Christian walk by choosing righteousness over evil ways, your unsaved relatives, friends and colleagues will look at you and say that you have become a fanatic. They say this because even at work, you are now hanging on to the Word of God by reading your Bible at lunch. To them, you are now strange.

I remember some of my relatives and a one-time close friend of mine getting together a couple of years after my salvation with an offer of a plane ticket to anywhere in the world that I wanted to go on a vacation so that I can have some rest and be cured of my new Christian zeal. They could make me such an offer because they had no idea of what I had found in Christ.

The Devil Crucified Jesus that Had No Sin

Jesus had no sin; meaning that He lived on earth for 33½ years without breaking any of God's commandments! Again, before Jesus came into the world, the devil had been very successful on earth in bringing death against people because everyone had a sin nature that we inherited from Adam. Also, Adam gave the devil his God-given authority and the devil was using it to enslave every human being on earth. God could not fully come to our defense against the devil because everyone had some form of sin or another in their lives that carried the judgment of death. The Lord Jesus came into the world without sin and as the Lamb chosen and prepared by God for Himself.

What is interesting is that when the foolish devil saw the Lord Jesus on earth, he decided that the Lord was bad for his business in the earth realm. Therefore, he wanted desperately to get rid of Him from the earth so that he can continue his wickedness on mankind without the Lord destroying his evil works. From the beginning, God the Father foresaw the devil's eagerness to destroy man (Jesus). Therefore, He came up with a salvation plan that He would immediately implement as soon as the devil goes after the Lord Jesus. God decided to catch the devil with his own evil hooks so, when the opportunity came for the devil to apprehend the Lord Jesus using the Jewish leaders and the Roman Judge, God the Father allowed him to go for it.

In other words, what the devil did not know was that God the Father, God the Son and God the Holy Spirit (the Godhead or Elohim) had already agreed that they would allow the devil to go after the Lord Jesus. When this happens, the Lord Jesus would go to the Cross for all men and then to hell to conquer the devil; death, the grave, all the evil principalities, all the evil powers, and take back the **Adamic Authority** that the devil stole from Adam in the Garden of Eden. <u>This plan was a hidden mystery by God the Father</u> according to **1 Corinthians 2:7-8:**

> "But we speak the **wisdom of God in a mystery, even the hidden wisdom**, which God ordained before the world unto our glory: *8* **Which none of the princes of this world** *(the devil and his agents)* **knew: for had they known it, they would not have crucified the Lord of glory**."

The devil lost it all when he foolishly went after the Lord Jesus.

Jesus Took the Blow of Death for All Believers
On the Cross, the Lord Jesus took the sting and the fear of death upon Himself for every man. He accomplished everything beautifully and successfully. As a result, death is an enemy today and is one of the things that you as a believer in Jesus Christ, do not have to fear anymore:

> **"The last enemy that shall be destroyed is death"** (1 Corinthians 15:26).

Even at the point of death, the Lord Jesus has absorbed the shock and the painful blow or impact of death for all who believe in Him. Again, you do not have to feel the sting of death anymore because as death is coming towards you with a dreadful and painful blow, the Christ in you rises up to absorb the impact for you! In other words, as you are going down in death, the "New Man" in you or the Christ in you is rising up.

It is a very quick and glorious exchange as you watch the Christ in you rise up just as death is about to deal its worst blow against you. He trades places with death for you and in you! **It is also at this point that the Christ in you for the first time has full expression as you see Him arising in you and standing in His full measure** the way it is written in **Ephesians 4:13:**

> "Till we all come in the unity of the faith, and of the knowledge of the Son of God, **unto a perfect man, <u>unto the measure of the stature of the fullness of Christ</u>."**

It was a most beautiful sight to see the 'Glorious Christ' rising up in me as I was taking my last breath. It is one of the times in our human and spiritual growth that a person can stand up as "a mighty warrior that is fully developed in Christ." This is why the Bible says that all creation is waiting for the manifestation of the sons of God. Even before we come to this stage of being fully developed in Christ, all creation groans for our manifestation as the sons of God. It desires to come to a place of glorious liberty as recorded in **Romans 8:19-23:**

> **"For the earnest expectation of the creature** *(creation)* **waiteth for the manifestation of the sons of God.** 20 For the creature was made subject to vanity, not willingly, but by reason of him who hath subjected the same in hope, 21 Because the creature itself also shall be delivered from the bondage of corruption into the glorious liberty of the children of God.
>
> 22 **For we know that the whole creation groaneth and travaileth in pain together until now.** 23 <u>And not only they, but ourselves also, which have the firstfruits of the Spirit,</u> **even we ourselves groan within ourselves, waiting for the adoption, to wit, the redemption of our body."**

God was willing to sacrifice His Son because He saw that He could bring sons and daughters to Himself in Christ; sons and daughters that do not just look like Christ but also act like Christ. This is why we are <u>daily</u> being conformed to the image of Christ. Thank God for placing us in Christ because no one can go before God if the person has not been conformed into the image of Christ — you must put on Christ!

In Summary of this chapter, I say that Christ is the one human being that has pleased God; has lived on earth and God says of Him, "I am well pleased with Him." As God's Lamb, He was without 'spot and blemish'. Also, when God looks at us believers today, He is pleased with us; but not because of what we are doing for Him but because of who He is in us and who He sees when He sees us; He looks at His Son in us.

It was the same way on the day that Adam and Eve sinned and God looked at Adam as he was giving Him excuses instead of repentance. Adam did not know that God was actually saying inwardly, "You do not even know what I have done in you; I have Me inside of you and if I was to deal with you according what you deserve, I would be harming Myself." Again, this was why He cursed the ground instead of cursing Adam directly.

Chapter 13
Jesus is the Strait and Narrow Gate

Definition of the Broad Way
Below are some of the definitions of the word **Broad**:
- **Wide in extent** from side to side; of great extent
- **Large in expanse**; spacious; of great breadth
- **Full; open**
- **Liberal; tolerant**: had broad views regarding social services
- **Not limited** or narrow

Many people that are caught up in the world's **broad way** (inside and outside of the Church) cast the scripture below behind them. They live their lives on their own terms and as a result, want everything to go their way. A lot of them are not aware that they are on the **broad way** while many do not care about the fact that they are on it as long as they make money:

> "Enter ye in at the strait gate: **for <u>wide is the gate,</u> and <u>broad is the way,</u> that leadeth to destruction,** and many there be which go in thereat" (Matthew 7:13).

Also, the Bible says in **Proverbs 14:12** that there is a way that seems broad; where everything goes your way but the end of it is death:

> "There is a way which seemeth right unto a man, **but the end thereof are the ways of death."**

We that are Christians cannot afford to walk on the **broad way** where everything goes our way and not God's way for us. One day, a lady asked me, *"Is everything going your way?"* My reply was *"I pray to God that it is not"* and she was shocked because the people of the world want everything to go their way. I then explained to her that my prayer is that nothing is going my own way but that everything is going the Lord's way for me. I added that those who live all their lives and do everything their own way instead of God's way for them, had better pray for 'their own created heaven' because their own way will not lead them to God or His heaven. As a matter of fact, their own way will lead them straight to hell.

Do not let the song about your life be; *"I Did It My Way."* God calls living for oneself and having everything go one's own way, **iniquity. This is a serious breach of the terms that God gave us as residents on His earth.** For example, when you look at a lot of people, you will notice that they married who they wanted to marry, they bought the house they wanted to buy, they worked wherever they wanted to work, and they did whatever they wanted to do; all on their own terms and God's will for them in these matters never even came into play in their decision making.

Also, when you speak to some of them, they will tell you that they do not have time for God, religion or people who talk religion. As a result, God is not a factor in their lives period. Some might even tell you that the Christian faith is nothing but superstitious beliefs and they chose to live their lives according to their own desires and definition of the 'right path' and of goodness. What do you think is going to happen to them on Judgment Day?

The Strait and Narrow Gate

On the other hand, God has a special **'Way'** prepared for us in Christ that is **"strait and narrow"** but the end of it is life according to **Matthew 7:14:**

> "Because **strait is the gate, and narrow is the way,** which leadeth unto life, and **few** there be that find it."

If you notice, the Bible does <u>not</u> say **straight** in the scripture above but **strait**. This is because there is a difference between them.

<u>Straight</u> is defined as:
1. Extending continuously in the same direction **without curving**: a straight line
2. Having **no waves or bends**: straight hair
3. **Not bent or bowed**; rigid or erect

Strait on the other hand is defined as:
- **A small road or opening**
- **A narrow channel**
- **A situation characterized by a specified degree of trouble or difficulty**
- **A position of difficulty, perplexity, distress, or need; stress**

In the definition above, **strait** has a certain degree of difficulty, distress or struggle. The reason God chose to use **Strait** is because He never told us that His way for us is nothing but a bed of roses; actually it is a rather difficult path. We are to individually locate this **Strait Gate** and walk in it and the way to do this is in Christ Jesus the Lord. To help us all avoid the fate that awaits all those that are on the **Broad Way** of life, the Lord Jesus came as our **"Strait and Narrow Gate"** that leads to life. He is our **Savoir** and only He (the **strait gate**) can lead a person **straight** to God the Father. This means that we must know Him and we must live our lives according to His Word. Again, when He was here, He declared the following in **John 14:6**:

> "...I am <u>the way</u>, the truth, and the life: no man cometh unto the Father, <u>but by me</u>."

Through the workings of the Holy Spirit, the Lord Jesus leads us on a daily basis as our **"Strait and Narrow Gate"** or **the Way**.

For God Almighty to be your God, the Word of God must have the preeminence in your life when you have a decision facing you. Therefore, before making any decision, you must know what the Word of God says about it so that your decision lines up with the Word of God. If you fail to do this and choose to go your own way by setting aside the Word of God, then, you are not the specimen that God is talking about in **Genesis 1:26**. He wants a man "after His likeness;"meaning a man that has His character by living according to His Word.

This is why when He spoke concerning David; He said that David was a man after His own heart that will do all His will in **Acts 13:22**. It is a testimony that God loves all those who do His will. This did not mean that David was perfect but that he made up his mind to live by God's Word; so whenever he sinned, he was quick to repent and to ask God for forgiveness:

> "And when he had removed him, <u>he raised up unto them David to be their king; to whom also he gave testimony, and said,</u> **I have found David the son of Jesse, a man after mine own heart, which shall fulfill all my will.**"

The problem is this: there is no way that anyone can do God's will if the person does not know what God's will is. **His will is found in His Word.** Therefore, if you are not seeking to know His Word, you will not do His will; even in the little things. The danger then becomes the fact that since you do not know and you cannot do His will in the little things; chances are that you will not seek Him in the big things either. This is the reason that the Word of God says that those who are faithful in the little things, will also be faithful in much and those who are unfaithful in little things, will be unfaithful in bigger things:

"He that is faithful in that which is least is faithful also in much: and <u>he that is unjust in the least is unjust also in much</u>" (Luke 16:10).

As a result, when God tries us, He gives us the little things first. What is sad is that there are some people that as soon as He gives them the little things, they immediately get a 'big head'. Therefore, the Lord makes sure that He has processed us very well in His ways before He releases the 'big things' that we are crying to Him for.

It is true that a walk with the Lord Jesus is a walk on the "**Strait and Narrow Gate,**" but we do develop a solid foundation to receive all that God wants to give us in our life time and at the end, we inherit eternal life. Praise the Lord!

Chapter 14
Jesus as the 'Seed of the Woman'

Jesus Bruised the Head of the Serpent

When Jesus was coming into the world, He knew that He was coming as the '**Seed of the Woman**' to "**bruise the head of the serpent**" as stated by God in **Genesis 3:14-15**:

> "And the LORD God said unto the serpent, Because thou hast done this, thou art cursed above all cattle, and above every beast of the field; upon thy belly shalt thou go, and dust shalt thou eat all the days of thy life: 15 And I will put enmity between thee and the woman, and between **thy seed** and **her seed; it shall bruise thy head,** <u>and thou shalt bruise his heel.</u>"

As we have already discussed, to do this; first, the Lord had to be a '**Perfect Lamb**' that is qualified as a bona fide <u>**man**</u> and whose blood is worthy to make atonement for our sins. Also, as '**the seed of the woman**' who is qualified to bruise the head of the serpent, the Lord Jesus had to demonstrate His obedience to God and He did it perfectly. Afterwards, the Lord went to war against the devil and all of his demons as recorded in **Colossians 2:15**:

> "**And having <u>spoiled</u> principalities and powers, <u>he made a shew of them openly,</u> triumphing over them in it.**"

The Lord Jesus "**bruised the head of the serpent;**" the devil and his cohorts known as principalities and powers. He triumphed victoriously over them openly; meaning that He disgraced them and He made a public spectacle of them after defeating them. He trampled the devil's head!

He truly "bruised the head of the serpent" and saved us, but <u>He also now and forever bears the marks of pierced</u>

<u>hands, feet and </u><u>side</u> as a reminder that <u>the serpent "bruised</u> <u>His heel"</u> because of us.

The Disobedience of One & the Obedience of One

We are told in **Romans 5:18-19** that the disobedience of Adam brought God's judgment of death upon humanity and through the obedience of Christ, God forgave us of our rebellion against Him:

> "Therefore as by the offence of one judgment
> came upon all men to condemnation; even so
> <u>by the righteousness of one</u> *(Jesus)* **the free gift**
> came upon all men unto justification of life.
> For as by one man's disobedience many were
> made sinners, so by the obedience of one shall
> many be made righteous."

The Lord Jesus not only demonstrated His 'perfect obedience' to God, He also demonstrated His bravery in rebuking the devil when he came to tempt Him. Unlike **Adam in the Garden of Eden, the Lord Jesus showed that man can overcome the forces of evil with the Word of God.** He took the kingdom back from the devil for us and as a result of His success in this mission, all that believe in His finished works on the Cross can now partake of His righteousness as revealed in **Romans 5:18-19** above.

God needed to bring all creation into His **set order** at the beginning and out of the **chaos** that Adam plunged the earth and its inhabitants into by his single act of rebellion. **God was the Lord over Adam while Adam was the Lord over the earth; so, when Adam rebelled against God, everything that Adam was in charge of, rebelled against him.** For example, before Adam's rebellion, the lions and all the wild animals had no aggression towards one another or towards man **but the minute Adam sinned against God, chaos set into everything that he was given dominion over.**

The reason for this is because the Bible says in **Isaiah 57:21** that, **"There is no peace to the wicked"** so, because of Adam's wickedness (rebellion), everything under him rebelled against him in retaliation. The earth also became a thorn in Adam's side as a harsh punishment.

Now, through the obedience of the Lord Jesus Christ, we are all justified by His blood before God. We should all be eternally grateful to the Lord Jesus for what He did for us.

The 'Seed of the Woman' *v.* the 'Unholy Trinity'

Understanding the 'seed of the woman' is one of the major areas that gave rise or birth to a lot of pagan religions. If you have heard of the 'unholy trinity' or 'false trinity' that is preached by some false or satanic organizations; well, this is their common root. Since God the Father judged the serpent in the Garden of Eden by saying to it that, "the seed of the woman shall bruise the head of the serpent (Genesis 3:15)," many societies and pagan religious leaders have sought to lay claim to being 'the seed of the woman' in their different generations.

In essence, the 'unholy trinity' is a belief that is the opposite of the Judeo-Christian belief in the **Godhead**; Father, Son and the Holy Spirit. The 'unholy trinity' belief is composed of satan, antichrist, and the false prophet. The devil has been using this belief system to stir up people in order to make them ascribe to themselves the power and position that is reserved only for God Almighty. For example, I wrote in one of my books titled, **Unveiling the God-mother** *(pages 69-79)* how the worship of the **'Sun-god'** and the **'Queen of Heaven'** began under the rulership of Nimrod; the great grandson of Noah. Nimrod began pagan worship on earth and his wife began the belief in the **'Unholy Trinity'**. Below is an excerpt of my writing in *Unveiling the God-mother* because Nimrod's wife was the originator of the God-mother. She started the belief of Nimrod being the sun-god, herself as the queen of heaven and their son –Damu as the prophesied 'seed of the woman:'

> *"Nimrod was the son of Cush, Cush was the son of Ham, and Ham was the son of Noah. He was the first person to rule the world and to establish human government in the "land of Nimrod" referred to in the Bible as Nineveh or Shinar. The Bible's record of him in* **Genesis 10:8-10** *is this:*
>
> > *'And Cush begat Nimrod; he began to be a mighty one in the earth. He was a mighty hunter before the Lord: wherefore it is said, Even as Nimrod the mighty hunter before the Lord. And the BEGINNING OF HIS KINGDOM WAS BABEL.'*
>
> *Nimrod was the first man to form an organized society with himself and his wife as the sole rulers. One Bible commentary in the Authorized King James Version gives the* **meaning of Nimrod as 'rebel.'** *The name* **Semiramis** *means* **'sea gift.'** *The name Babylon comes from his city,* **Babel!**
>
> *Legend has it that Nimrod brought home a strange woman (Semiramis) as his wife after one of his hunting expeditions. He then devised a plan to conceal her true identity. He explained to his subjects that she actually came out of the sea. He told them that she was an offspring of the sea-god (half-man and half-fish pagan sea-god) and man! Therefore, her name meant 'a gift of the sea.' This is how Nimrod began the legend of the female* **'half-woman and half-fish'** *known in the western world as the* **mermaid** *and in the Bible as* **Ashtoreth.**
>
> *Nimrod gave Semiramis the platform to control religious activities in his kingdom because of the story he built around her. Semiramis' true identity, according to tradition is that she was actually a prostitute with whom Nimrod became*

fascinated and married. Queen Semiramis was in full control of the religious systems in Babylon. She plotted Nimrod's destruction when she became pregnant due to adultery and King Nimrod threatened to reveal her true identity/origin, expose her adultery, and dethrone her.

*It is stated that she had King Nimrod torn to pieces by her religious priests after she gave them her specially prepared 'drink', and her bastard son Damu was made king. **Semiramis then deified herself as the mother of the god Damu and she also became known as the "the queen of heaven."** Thus, Semiramis originated the goddess system of pagan religions."*

Not only is she the originator of the 'god-mother', she is also the originator of the **worship of mother and child**. All forms of pagan worship on earth began with the rule of Nimrod and his wife because all humanity was under their rule at the time. Even after God confounded and scattered all the people to different parts of the earth, they took the pagan worship or idolatry that Nimrod and his wife taught them with them. I wrote about this in the first of these series of books titled, ***Experiencing the Depths of God the Father,*** pages 105-106. Below is an excerpt:

*"According to **Flavius Josephus** in his book titled, Antiquities of the Jews, Nimrod heard about the flood that took place in the days of his great great-grandfather Noah and he became angry with God because of it. Nimrod was very much anti-God and the following is Josephus' account of Nimrod and his work:*

*'2. (113) **Now it was Nimrod who excited them to such an affront and contempt of God.** He was the grandson of Ham, the son of Noah, a bold man, and of great strength of hand. He persuaded them to ascribe it to God, as if it was through his (Nimrod's) means that they were happy, but to believe that it was their own courage which procured that happiness.*

(114) He also gradually changed the government into tyranny, seeing no other way out of turning men from the fear of God, but to bring them into a constant dependence on his power.

He also said he would be avenged in God, if he should have a mind to drown the world again: for he would build a tower too high for the waters to be able to reach: and that he would avenge himself on God for destroying their forefathers. *3. (115)* <u>**Now the multitude were very ready to follow the determination of Nimrod and to esteem it a piece of cowardice to submit to God;**</u> **and they built a tower, neither sparing any pain, nor being in any degree negligent about the work;** *and, by reason of multitude of hands employed in it, it grew very high, sooner than anyone could expect.'*

*From the above writing by Josephus, you can see Nimrod's rationale for building the Tower of Babel. Nimrod was ignorant of God's promise to Noah that He would never flood the earth again and he also never bothered to find out the covenant that God made with Noah and all living things that was signified by the Rainbow. As a result, he embarked on a rebellious path taking everyone that was subject to him in his kingdom with him on the same path. His zeal and determination prompted the Godhead (**Elohim**) to get together again in counsel to determine what to do about the rebellion that they saw in Nimrod and his subjects."*

Jesus as the Judge of the Living and the Dead

The Lord Jesus is now the Judge of all who are alive and all that are dead. On Judgment Day, He is going to sit and judge every human being based on how well they obeyed the Word of God while they were alive. This is why He told us that the Father will not judge anyone but that the Father has committed all judgments to Him according to **John 5:22-29:**

"For the Father judgeth no man, but hath committed all judgment unto the Son: *23* That all men should honour the Son, even as they honour the Father. He that honoureth not the Son honoureth not the Father which hath sent him… *26* For as the Father hath life in himself; so hath he given to the Son to have life in himself;

27 **And hath given him authority to execute judgment also, because he is the Son of man.** *28* **Marvel not at this: for the hour is coming, in the which all that are in the graves shall hear his voice,** *29* **And shall come forth; they that have done good, unto the resurrection of life; and they that have done evil, unto the resurrection of damnation."**

As we saw in a previous chapter, the one thing that is certain is that, the ungodly or the wicked will never have the pleasure of seeing the glorious face of God the Father. They will not even be able to withstand the glory that radiates or emanates from Him because of their sin nature. As a result, it is God's Son (the Lord Jesus Christ) that deals directly with mankind through the Holy Spirit. The LORD Jesus as part of the Godhead is also very Holy but God placed GRACE and MERCY in Him for all humanity. If you revisit the scriptures that detail the encounters that people like Abraham, Moses, Joshua, Manoah and others had with the LORD Jesus as either **LORD, the Angel of the LORD, the Captain of the LORD's Hosts** or **the LORD of Hosts** in the Old Testament, you will notice that they always shielded or covered their faces because of God's glory and holiness. His glory and holiness are such that when you are in His presence, you feel so guilty, so dirty, so unworthy, and very unclean as you become aware of your own shortcomings. That is how holy He is when you see Him as God. At the same time, you are aware of God's incredible mercy and love for you.

It is amazing the impact and effect of rebellion on a person. It leaves a person naked and defeated by evil spirits. God the Father once told me that, "Rebellion cannot put down rebellion." It confirms what is written in **2 Corinthians 10:6:**

> "And having in a readiness to revenge all disobedience, **when your obedience is fulfilled.**"

This was why in order to judge and bruise the head of the serpent (the devil); the Lord Jesus saw to it that He perfectly obeyed God the Father. **I remember once asking the Lord why we do not see the greater works that He promised that we will do after He went back to heaven.** His reply to me was, *"My children have so many doors opened to the devil in their lives that if I should unleash them against the devil the way that they ask me to, the devil will take many of them out with just one visit."* According to Him, the key to shutting these open doors to the devil in our lives is obedience.

There is a saying that, **"Two wrongs cannot make a right."** The same is true in the realm of the spirit; two wrongs cannot make a right there also. This is why when we come before God in prayer, we are to first worship Him, glorify Him, praise Him and then, ask Him to forgive all our transgressions. It is only when we have fulfilled this aspect of our fellowship with God that we can turn around and begin to rebuke the devil and all his fellow rebellious spirits.

Finding a 'non-rebellious person' was the problem in the vision that God showed the Apostle John in **Revelation 5:1-7** concerning the **'book'** with the **"Seven Seals"** that no man in heaven and on earth was found worthy to open but the Lord Jesus. **Only the Lord Jesus could open it because He is the only human being that has never rebelled against God or His Word:**

> "And I saw in the right hand of him that sat on the throne a book written within and on

the backside, sealed with seven seals. 2 And I saw a strong angel proclaiming with a loud voice, Who is worthy to open the book, and to loose the seals thereof? 3 **And no man in heaven, nor in earth, neither under the earth, was able to open the book, neither to look thereon.** 4 And I wept much, because no man was found worthy to open and to read the book, neither to look thereon.

5 **And one of the elders saith unto me, Weep not: behold, the Lion of the tribe of Juda, the Root of David, hath prevailed to open the book, and to loose the seven seals thereof.** 6 And I beheld, and, lo, in the midst of the throne and of the four beasts, and in the midst of the elders, stood a Lamb as it had been slain, having seven horns and seven eyes, which are the seven Spirits of God sent forth into all the earth. 7 And **he came and took the book out of the right hand of him that sat upon the throne.**"

What you see in the scripture above is how horrible man's situation was before the coming of the Lord Jesus. It was really sad that nobody in heaven, on earth or under earth was worthy to be used by God as His instrument of judgment against the rebels because all humanity was in disobedience or rebellion against God since Adam. **Therefore, the Apostle John said that he "wept much" because there was no one to rise up to pronounce judgment on God's behalf or that can exercise dominion on God's behalf.** An elder in heaven then consoled John by telling Him about the **"Lion of the Tribe of Judah"** that had prevailed and is **worthy** to take the **'Book'** and to **open** the **"Seven Seals"** of judgments.

The Lord Jesus went down in death as the **Lamb of God** but He rose **victoriously** as the **"LION OF THE TRIBE OF JUDAH!"** Therefore, God the Father has committed all judgments to Him and He has successfully judged the "prince of this world, the devil" as stated in **John 16:11** that the "the prince of this world is judged."

The Lord Jesus told the disciples that we are going to sit with Him and that we are also going to judge the wicked. Just think about it; we are going to judge these demons that are troubling us today. It will be our job as **joint-heirs with Christ** to judge the wicked spirits and wicked men and women for what they did to us and for what they did to God's creation. Hallelujah!:

> "Do ye not know that **the saints shall judge the world?** and if the world shall be judged by you, are ye unworthy to judge the smallest matters?" (1 Corinthians 6:2).

The **'Book'** with the Seven Seals that was revealed to John is of great interest to us because this is not the first time that this book is mentioned in scriptures. Let us now take a look at it before we move on. A **'Book'** was shown to the Apostle John in the vision that he narrated in **Revelation 5:1-7. He saw the Lord Jesus as the "Lamb that was slain" and as the only person in heaven and on earth qualified to approach the <u>Throne</u> and <u>He that sat on it</u>, to take the 'Book' out of His hand.** We first saw this **'Book'** that John is talking about here in **Ezekiel 2:8-10** because the Prophet Ezekiel was also given a vision that revealed the nature of this **'Book'** in his days. Below is what he wrote about God's revelation to him about it:

> "But thou, son of man, hear what I say unto thee; <u>Be not thou rebellious like that rebel-lious house:</u> open thy mouth, and eat that I give thee *(obedience to God's Word).* 9 And when I looked, behold, an hand was sent unto me; **and, lo, a roll of a <u>book</u> was therein; 10 And he spread it before me; and it was written within**

and without: and there was written therein lamentations, and mourning, and woe."

As soon as the **'Book'** was opened, the different judgments began to come forth even as the Prophet Ezekiel was shown — lamentations, mourning and woes. The **'Book'** is revealing what will happen at the very last days; how God will pour out His Judgments on all rebels through His Son Jesus Christ. **To put it in simpler terms, it is a 'Book' that contains the judgments that God has for all those who rebelled against Him.**

Again, it took someone who was perfectly obedient to the Word of God i.e., one who had not rebelled again the Word of God to lose the seals and give the order for judgments on rebels to begin. **We have already seen how that the Lord Jesus after becoming the 'Perfect Lamb' of God, also became the Righteous Judge of all.** At the time that John was being shown this vision in **Revelation 5:1-7**, the Lord Jesus had already gone to hell and had taken back all authority that satan stole from Adam. He had also collected the keys to death, hell and the grave as stated in **Revelation 1:18:**

> **"I am he that liveth, and was dead; and, behold, I am alive for evermore, Amen; and have the keys of hell and of death."**

After taking away the authority and keys from the devil, He told His disciples go into all the world and preach the Good News of His resurrection (the Gospel) to every creature in **Mark 16:15-18:**

> **"And he said unto them, Go ye into all the world, and preach the gospel to every creature.** *16* **He that believeth and is baptized shall be saved; but he that believeth not shall be damned.** *17* And these signs shall follow them that believe; In my name shall they cast out devils; they shall

> speak with new tongues; 18 **They shall take up
> serpents; and <u>if they drink any deadly thing,
> it shall not hurt them</u>; they shall lay hands on
> the sick, and they shall recover."**

According to the scripture above, He said that even poison will not have any deadly effect on us; when we drink or eat poison unknowingly, it will be powerless against us.

We know that the Lord has given to all who believe in Him the power to heal the sick, speak with new tongues, cleanse the lepers and raise the dead. He also gave us the **authority to tread upon serpents and scorpions** (devils and demons) **and over all the power of the devil himself** *(the enemy)* because He gained victory over the devil for us and He has taken away the power that the devil had over humanity:

> **"Behold, I give unto you <u>power to tread on
> serpents and scorpions</u>, and <u>over all the power
> of the enemy</u>: and nothing shall by any means
> hurt you"** (Luke 10:19).

What all these tell us is that we should not allow the devil to illegally lord it over us in any area of our lives because the Lord Jesus has forever defeated him for us. We have been commissioned by the Lord to cast him out, to tread him under foot and walk all over his power. He cannot harm us if we exercise our faith in Christ and live by the Word of God. This does not mean that you can foolishly go and get a snake and play around with it until it bits you so that you can put this scripture to test as some have done and have died. We are not to tempt God.

In the next chapter, we are going to look at how God the Father acknowledged the Lord Jesus as both **LORD** and **GOD**.

Chapter 15
Jesus as LORD and GOD

God the Father Acknowledged Jesus as Both LORD and GOD

God the Father did not just **anoint** the Lord Jesus, He also made Him **LORD** and **GOD**; a **co-equal** with God the Father and God the Holy Spirit in the **Godhead.** This is revealed to us in **Hebrews 1:8-12:**

> "But unto the **Son** *(Jesus)* **he** *(God the Father)* **saith, Thy throne, O God, is forever and ever: a sceptre of righteousness is the sceptre of thy kingdom.** 9 Thou hast loved righteousness, and hated iniquity; therefore God, even thy God *(God the Father)*, hath anointed thee *(Jesus)* with the oil of gladness above thy fellows *(humanity)*.
>
> 10 And, **Thou, Lord** *(Jesus)*, in the beginning hast laid the foundation of the earth; and the heavens are the works of thine hands: *(the Word of God)* 11 they shall perish; but thou remainest *(eternal)*; and they all shall wax old as doth a garment; 12 And as a vesture shalt thou fold them up, and they shall be changed: **but thou art the same, and thy years shall not fail**."

This scripture above shows us the eternal age of Christ and those that are in Him — 33 1/2 years forever! Also, you can show it to someone who has difficulty believing that the Lord Jesus is both **LORD** and **GOD**. It will clearly show them what **God the Father** said about **God the Son**. In other words, you can safely say that the Lord Jesus temporarily stopped being a part the **Godhead** for a season to become a human being but He regained His status upon getting back to heaven.

Therefore, the event that is revealed in **Hebrews 1:8-12** above took place on the day that <u>God the Father</u> formally <u>re-enthroned His Son and anointed Him</u> as both **LORD** and **GOD** *(received Him back as part of the Godhead)*. We refer to this day on earth as the <u>Day of Pentecost</u>. Actually, <u>in the spirit realm</u>, this event happened thousands of years before it was manifested on earth on the **Day of Pentecost.**

By the single act of taking His own blood into heaven and into the Holy of Holies on our behalf, the Lord Jesus became our High Priest. Therefore, God the Father had to pour the anointing oil upon Him as it is required in the installation of a new High Priest. <u>It was the overflow of the anointing on the Lord Jesus as our High Priest (head of the Church) that the believers received on earth on the **Day of Pentecost**</u>. We see in **Psalm 133:2:**

> **"It is like the precious <u>ointment upon the head, that ran down upon the beard, even Aaron's beard</u>** *(the High Priest)***: that went down to the skirts of his garments** *(his body i.e., the Church).***"**

The Lord Jesus' role on our behalf as our **LORD, God,** and **High Priest** was formally activated or implemented in both heaven and earth on the **Day of Pentecost.** This is why the oil with which He was anointed overflowed into the earth realm! God the Father confirmed His Son as **LORD, God,** and **High Priest** by telling Him, **"Thy throne, O God...and Thou, Lord..."**as we saw in **Hebrews 1:8-12.**

From this day on, the Lord Jesus regained His former and legitimate title as **LORD** and **God** in both heaven and on earth. **Because He also defeated the devil and took back the authority that Adam gave him, the devil is no longer a legitimate authority in the lives of all those who believe in the Lordship of Jesus Christ.** The Lord Jesus is now the legitimate authority on earth forever.

Again, although the Lord Jesus had been part of the **Godhead** in all of eternity, He was sent to the earth by His Father to be the **Savior** of humanity. **As a result, He temporarily stepped down as part of the Godhead and took on the nature of a bona fide man** as stated in **Philippians 2:7:**

> "**...And** took upon him the form of a servant, and was made in the likeness of men."

From what we have seen so far, you can now understand that the identity of the Lord Jesus is deeper than what the Pharisees and the scribes thought Him to be when He was here. If you will take the time to let God the Father reveal Him to you, you too will see for yourself that the Lord Jesus was not 'off His rocker' when He said that before Abraham was, "**I Am;**" meaning that He is God. He can say this because **He is the very Word that God the Father spoke** and as God the Father Himself puts it, *"A man and his word are one."*

King David's Revelation of Jesus' Lordship

King David had a revelation of the identity of the Lord Jesus as is evidenced in his writings in the book of Psalms. In **Psalm 110:1-4** for example, **you can see his revelation of how God the Father spoke to God the Son**; He called Him Lord:

> "**The LORD said unto my Lord,** *(God the Father speaking to God the Son)* **Sit thou at my right hand, until I make thine enemies thy footstool.** 2 The LORD shall send the rod of thy strength out of Zion: rule thou in the midst of thine enemies.
>
> 3 <u>Thy people shall be willing in the day of thy power, in the beauties of holiness from the womb of the morning: thou hast the dew of thy youth</u>. 4 <u>The LORD hath sworn, and will not</u>

<u>repent, Thou art a priest for ever after the order of Melchizedek."</u>

What the above scriptures tell us is that King David had a revelation of how God's Son (who is also Lord) is sitting at the right hand of God the Father. He was able to relay the conversation between God the Father and His Son, Jesus Christ the Lord. God the Father told God the Son that He has set Him in a position of power (right hand) and that He has given Him victory over all His enemies. He also made the Lord Jesus as an everlasting (High) Priest like Melchizedek.

Jesus as LORD God

It was prophesied in **Isaiah 7:14** that God will actually come to dwell with His people Israel but the people did not recognize that the Lord Jesus was the fulfillment of the prophecy:

"...The Lord himself shall give you a sign; <u>Behold, a virgin shall conceive, and bear a son, and shall call his name **Immanuel**</u> *(meaning God with us)."*

As you will see in the scripture below, the Lord Jesus did not rebuke the disciple Thomas when he called Him **"My Lord and my God"** in **John 20:26-29:**

"And after eight days again his disciples were within, and Thomas with them: **then came Jesus, the doors being shut, and stood in the midst, and said, Peace be unto you.** 27 <u>Then saith he to Thomas, Reach hither thy finger, and behold my hands; and reach hither thy hand, and thrust it into my side: and be not faithless, but believing.</u> 28 **And Thomas answered and said unto him, <u>My Lord and my God.</u>** 29 Jesus saith unto him,

Thomas, because thou hast seen me, thou hast believed: blessed are they that have not seen, and yet have believed."

The Lord Jesus Himself acknowledged that He is both **LORD** and **God** as we see in **John 13:13** below:

"Ye call me Master and <u>Lord</u>: and ye say well; for so <u>I am</u>."

He has the combined title and position of both **LORD** and **God** (**LORD God**) but not everyone is willing to accept Him as **LORD God**; even in the Church today. A lot of people in the Church only pay Him 'lip service' because their actions constantly demonstrate that Jesus is not their **LORD God** and that they are the captains of their own lives. The truth is that for the **Lord** to be your **LORD God**, you have to willingly surrender yourself to His **Lordship** by obeying His Word in every area of your life. Look at what he said to those who pay Him 'lip service':

"And why call ye me, Lord, Lord, and do not the things which I say? *47* <u>Whosoever cometh to me, and</u> **hereth my sayings, and doeth them,** <u>I will shew you to whom he is like:</u> *48* **He is like a man which built an house, and digged deep, and laid the foundation on a rock: and when the flood arose, the stream beat vehemently upon that house, and could not shake it: for it was founded upon a rock.**

49 **But** <u>he that heareth, and doeth not</u>**, is like a man that without a foundation built an house upon the earth; against which the stream did beat vehemently, and immediately it fell; and the ruin of that house was great"** (Luke 6:46-49).

It Takes the Holy Spirit to Call Jesus LORD

The Bible tells us in **1 Corinthians 12:3** that no one can say that Jesus is Lord but by the help of the Holy Spirit. As a result, it takes the Holy Spirit to help you confess Jesus as your Lord and to relate to Him as such:

> "Wherefore I give you to understand, that no man speaking by the Spirit of God calleth Jesus accursed: **and that no man can say that Jesus is the Lord, but by the Holy Ghost.**"

Also, the Lord Jesus said in **John 15:5** that without Him, we are not able to do anything. We need Him even to become Christians:

> "I am the vine, ye are the branches: He that abideth in me, and I in him, the same bringeth forth much fruit: **for without me ye can do nothing.**"

The Lord Jesus' Humility as God

The Bible tells us in **Philippians 2:5-11** that the Lord Jesus did not consider it a big deal to be equal with God but instead, He chose to humble Himself; meaning that He submitted Himself to God the Father. He obeyed God in everything; even when God the Father told Him to go to the Cross and die for our sins. Let us look at the scripture below because it shows how humble the Lord Jesus really is as both **LORD** and **God:**

> "Let this mind be in you, which was also in Christ Jesus: 6 **Who, being in the form of God, thought it not robbery to be equal with God:** 7 **But made himself of no reputation, and took upon him the form of a servant, and was made in the likeness of men:** 8 **And**

being found in fashion as a man, he humbled himself, and became obedient unto death, even the death of the cross.

9 Wherefore God also hath highly exalted him, and given him a name which is above every name: 10 That at the name of Jesus every knee should bow, of things in heaven, and things in earth, and things under the earth; 11 And that every tongue should confess that Jesus Christ is Lord, to the glory of God the Father."

Do not let anybody tell you that Jesus is not God because He is both **LORD** and **God** and He is humble about it!

Chapter 16
Jesus as the Genuine King of Israel

The Children of Israel Asked God for a King

After the death of the last High Priest named Eli, God raised up Samuel as both a Prophet and a Judge in Israel but after several years, the children of Israel demanded to have a king over them instead of Samuel. In response to their demand, God appointed Saul as the first King and when He removed Saul as the King, He raised up David as the second King in Israel. After the reign of King David, the children of Israel came under the reigns of various kings. These kings began to appoint priests and high priests of their choice to preside over religious affairs in Israel until they went into captivity in Babylon.

Mark Anthony Made Herod King Over Israel

After their return from captivity, the children of Israel no longer had kings but priests and high priests. This continued until right before the time of the Lord Jesus when after the death of Julius Caesar in Rome, **Marcus Antonius** *(Mark Anthony)* appointed **Herod** as a **King** in Israel against the will of the Jewish people. You can read about this in the writings of **Flavius Josephus'**, *Jewish Antiquities:*

> *"Hereupon **Antony**, by reason of the old hospitable friendship he had made with his father [**Antipater**-Herod's father], at that time when he was with Gabinius, **he made both Herod and Phasaelus tetrarchs** (Kings), **and <u>committed the public affairs of the Jews to them</u>**, and wrote letters to that purpose"* (Book 14, Chapter 13:1).

Herod was made a King by Mark Anthony and Octavia (Caesar Augustus) because Herod as a mercenary soldier helped them to hunt for Caesar's killers (Brutus and Cassius). His kingship was nothing but a reward for serving Rome. What this means is that King Herod was not a genuine

Jewish King but a puppet of Rome. As a result, the Jewish people refused to give him the honor of a true Jewish King. **Therefore, King Herod** hated the fact that **a genuine Jewish King** had been born in Bethlehem when he heard about the birth of the Lord Jesus from the "wise men" —**Matthew 2:1-8:**

> "Now when Jesus was born in Bethlehem of Judaea in the days of Herod the king, behold, there came wise men from the east to Jerusalem,
> 2 Saying, **Where is he that is born King of the Jews? for we have seen his star in the east, and are come to worship him.** 3 When Herod the king had heard these things, he was troubled, and all Jerusalem with him.
>
> 4 And when he had gathered all the chief priests and scribes of the people together, **he demanded of them where Christ should be born.** 5 And they said unto him, In Bethlehem of Judaea: for thus it is written by the prophet, 6 **And thou Bethlehem, in the land of Juda, art not the least among the princes of Juda: for out of thee shall come a Governor, that shall rule my people Israel.**
>
> 7 Then Herod, when he had privily called the wise men, enquired of them diligently what time the star appeared. 8 And he sent them to Bethlehem, and said, Go and search diligently for the young child; and when ye have found him, bring me word again, that I may come and worship him also."

Also, we learned in **Matthew 2:16** that King Herod immediately sought to kill the new born King (Jesus) by commanding that all the male children born at the time of the Lord's birth be killed with no exception:

> "Then Herod, when he saw that he was mocked of the wise men, was exceeding wroth, **and**

sent forth, and slew all the children that were
in Bethlehem, and in all the coasts thereof,
from two years old and under, according to
the time which he had diligently enquired
of the wise men."

To protect the infant Jesus, God the Father sent Him, his
mother Mary and Joseph to Egypt and brought Him back
after the death of King Herod. Joseph and Mary decided
to make their home in Galilee and because the Lord Jesus
was raised in Galilee, the Jewish leaders of His days never
saw Him beyond being 'a man from Galilee'. According
to them, not only was He from Galilee; to make matters
worse, no prophet had ever come from Galilee. We see this
recorded in **John 7:50-53:**

"Nicodemus saith unto them, (he that came
to Jesus by night, being one of them,) 51 <u>Doth
our law judge any man, before it hear him, and
know what he doeth</u>? 52 <u>They answered and
said unto him</u>, **Art thou also of Galilee? Search,
and look: <u>for out of Galilee ariseth no prophet</u>.**
53 And every man went unto his own house."

Jesus Acted Like No Earthly King Ever Could
Although the Lord Jesus never sat on an earthly throne
during His time here on earth, nonetheless, He acted and
spoke as no King on earth ever could. Also, when He received
worship as the **"Son of David,"** the Jewish leaders knew that
it meant Jesus was functioning as the **Eternal King of Israel**
foretold by the prophets. This was why one of the accusations
that they had against Him was that He claimed to be the **'King
of the Jews'** in **John 18:33-38:**

"<u>Then Pilate entered into the judgment hall again,
and called Jesus, and said unto him</u>, **Art thou the
King of the Jews?** 34 Jesus answered him, **Sayest**

thou this thing of thyself, or did others tell it thee of me? *35* Pilate answered, **Am I a Jew? Thine own nation and the chief priests have delivered thee unto me:** what hast thou done…?

37 Pilate therefore said unto him, **Art thou a king then?** Jesus answered, **Thou sayest that I am a king.** To this end was I born, and for this cause came I into the world, that I should bear witness unto the truth. Every one that is of the truth heareth my voice. *38* Pilate saith unto him, What is truth?…"

As recorded in **Matthew 27:29**, before the Lord's crucifixion, the Jewish leaders and even the soldiers mocked Him because they did not believe that He was truly the **King of the Jews:**

"And when they had platted a **crown of thorns, they put it upon his head,** and **a reed in his right hand:** and they bowed the knee before him, and mocked him, saying, Hail, King of the Jews."

Even after His crucifixion, they wrote the accusation against Him on a plaque and nailed it to His Cross. They accused Him of claiming to be the **'King of the Jews'** —Matthew 27:37:

"And set up over his head his accusation written, **THIS IS JESUS THE KING OF THE JEWS.**"

The Jewish leader meant nailing the plaque of the accusation against the Lord Jesus to His Cross to be a sign of humiliation and victory over Him, but on the 3rd day after His death, He rose again victoriously. His resurrection confirmed the truth that He is indeed, the **King of the Jews. As a result, the Lord Jesus is now and forever the only King in Israel that sits on the throne of His earthly father King David and He rules the earth from heaven!**

Chapter 17
Jesus Came to Help Us Put a Face to God

Seeing Jesus is Beholding God in the Flesh
From the beginning of His dealings with the children of Israel, God forbade them from making any graven image of Him or setting up anything that represents Him or His likeness. In other words, no image is to be made to depict God or His likeness. This is why the children of Israel never had anything that showed them what God looked like. Therefore, **Hebrews 1:1-3** talks about how the Lord Jesus came to help us put a face to God.

When God the Father sent His Son into the world, He made sure that we were all made aware that His Son came to show us what He Himself looks like. **As a result, beholding the Lord Jesus was beholding God the Father in the flesh:**

> "God, who at sundry times and in divers manners spake in time past unto the fathers by the prophets, 2 **Hath in these last days spoken unto us by his Son,** whom he hath appointed heir of all things, by whom also he made the worlds; 3 **Who being the brightness of his glory, and the express image of his person,** and upholding all things by the word of his power, **when he had by himself purged our sins, sat down on the right hand of the Majesty on high.**"

The scripture above also confirms what is written in Psalm 110:1-2 that we saw earlier; when God the Father said unto the Lord Jesus, His Son, sit at my right hand and let me fight your enemies for you. The battle of course, is the salvation of man from the devil's enslavement and the Lord had to go through death and into hell for mankind.

Remember our previous discussion in *Chapter 10* of how the disciple named Philip said to the Lord Jesus, "show us the Father and we will be satisfied?" The Lord's response to him was, "have I been with you this long and you still do not know me?" **He then told Philip that he that has seen Him has seen the Father** in **John 14:7-11**.

Therefore, we can safely say that **the Lord Jesus came to help us put a face to God the Father because He is <u>the express or manifested image of God.</u>** If you want to know what God the Father looks or acts like, all you have to do is, take a look at the Lord Jesus. The Lord Jesus came to **demonstrate or reveal** the face of God to us and He told us so in **Matthew 11:27:**

> "All things are delivered unto me of my Father: and no man knoweth the Son, but the Father; **neither knoweth any man the Father, save the Son, and <u>he to whomsoever the Son will reveal him</u>**."

And also in **John 1:18:**

> "**No man hath seen God at any time; the only begotten Son, which is in the bosom of the Father, <u>he hath declared him</u>**."

The Lord Jesus' coming to help us put a face to God is summarized thus in **1 Timothy 3:16:**

> "... **God was manifest in the flesh**, justified in the Spirit, seen of angels, preached unto the Gentiles, believed on in the world, received up into glory."

The Danger of Having Images of Angels and Others Things

Today, God still does not like it when people setup

any statues, images of angels, crosses and other things that some Christians are ignorantly passionate about. **I remember asking God the Father why He does not want us to have graven images or a representation of Him or angels. His reply was that when He formed man; He took clay from the earth and He spat upon it and molded it into an image. Because He is God, He was able to give the image life by breathing into it. Therefore, graven or molded images such as figurines of angels, or other beings (be it in heaven or on earth), speak of creation.**

When someone makes a little or a big figurine of an angel for instance, because the person is not God, the person does not have the ability to give that figurine or image life. **The danger that stems from graven images is that when the person places the image (made or bought) in his or her house, <u>the image then becomes a vacuum that needs to be filled with life</u>. Because the person is not able to give it life, guess who then comes or sends his demons to occupy the vacuum that the image represents — the devil!** <u>The reason he can come is because creating the image or statue was in disobedience to God's Word that you should not create it or buy it</u>. Setting up the image in your home then becomes a direct invitation to the devil and his demons.

Also, because the devil knows that you are in rebellion against God's Word about graven images, him and his demons can occupy that graven image and from it, vex you and your family with all types of afflictions. While in these statues, they can manifest certain acts like making the statues to bleed in their efforts to convince the people to leave the statues in place, to worship or to reverence the statues. He loves it when people get involved in idolatry through graven images.

Today, there are a lot of Christians that have all kinds of graven angels in their yards, inside their houses, in their bedrooms, and everywhere they can put them and the devil goes, "thank you very much for giving me a little place to inhabit in your home; it speaks of creation but you cannot give it life so I will come help you out." As a result, when the devil wants to afflict people in the home, all he has to do as they pass by the graven image is, breathe something against them and one by one, members of that family can be afflicted and made sick.

In essence, graven images speak of creation and the only time that God told a person to create a graven image was when He instructed Moses to build the Ark of the Covenant. He also told him to create two <u>Cherubims</u> (graven images) facing each other and to place them on either side of the Mercy Seat on top of the Ark but guess what happened? <u>God himself came and dwelt between these two Cherubims as the life inside the Holy of Holies!</u> So, when you setup your graven little angels, it might seem like nothing but in the realm of the spirit, it speaks volumes because you are asking for life for it. Since you cannot put life into it, the devil will then come to put things like: weariness, fatigue, insomnia, lethargy, sicknesses, diseases, death, etc., into it for you.

My Personal Encounters with Demons in Angel Statues
Experience #1:

Some years ago, I was part of an evangelism group and on some Saturday mornings, we went out to minister the Gospel in different neighborhoods. One day, we met a woman and her daughter in one of the apartment complexes as they were walking home and we ministered the Gospel to both of them. When we were done, they both received the Lord and were very happy. The woman told us not to go just yet because she had a teenage son at home that she wanted us to minister the Gospel to as well. We followed her home and sure enough, her son was home and we ministered the

Gospel to him and he also received the Lord as his Savior. After about a year, we decided to revisit the apartment complex as we normally do concerning the places that we had been before. Therefore, we came to the lady's complex and on the way to her particular apartment, I began to smell a very unnatural foul odor and I knew that it was a spiritual smell. There was also a very heavy oppression; almost as though a house was sitting on my head. I asked the Lord what it all meant but I heard nothing back from Him. When we knocked on the door, the lady came to door and invited us in and immediately, I was almost suffocating because of the foul odor. I was stunned as I looked at the apartment and it was very clean physically but the foul odor was heavy in her apartment and I knew that the source of it was in her apartment.

Also, as soon as she realized that we were the people that had ministered to her a year before, she began to cry. We asked her what was wrong and she told us that her husband had left her and quite naturally, we wanted to know why. She asked if we remembered her son that we led to the Lord a year prior and we said yes. She then informed us that he ran away from home and that her husband blamed her for it and as a result, has left her. We all decided that the best thing to do was to pray for her, her husband and her son but meanwhile, I was still struggling with the unnatural foul odor.

*Unknown to me was that she had **a very little statue of an angel** on her bookshelf in the livingroom, but the minute we closed our eyes to pray, **the little statue of an angel sprang up!** I could see it in the realm of the spirit with two cymbals in her hands and she was clanging them in her attempt to drown out our prayers. I was shocked and I opened my eyes to look at the book shelf and I saw that **the little statue of an angel was not bigger than the size of a perfume bottle.** My thought was; how can something so small have any power.*

*Then, the Lord spoke to me saying, **"This little statue of an angel is housing the spirit that has come to scatter this family. It may look small but the demon in it is not."** I did not want to scare the woman so all I could do was to pray that the Lord will give her a serious dislike for the **little statue of an angel** so that she can throw it out.*

Experience #2:
*I went to visit a fellow Christian one day, and she had a **big statue of an angel** in their yard. As I was making my way to her front door, the demon in the angel statue by the front door spewed some foul odor at me as I was passing by it to climb the steps leading up to the front door. I turned in anger and said to it, **"I rebuke you in the name of the Lord Jesus. I did not set you up and the Bible says that 'everywhere the sole of my foot treads upon is mine'. Therefore, I bind you with chains and fetters of iron"** and I quarantined it to its space for the entire length of my visit.*

*I told it to be still throughout my visit and I sent its wickedness back to it. I was not willing to go home sick just because I went to see someone. **I could not cast it out of the yard because it was not my place to do so. It was given permission to be there by the owner of the house.** The truth is that people have a right to setup **containers to house demons** if that is what they want but the demons do not have my permission to afflict me when I pass by.*

I shared the above experiences with you so that those who are passionate about their graven images of angels, animals and other objects will know what they are allowing into their lives and into their homes. Some people even wear them as pendants and broaches. How sad and how ignorant that Christians will do these things. They represent nothing but evil covenants with the devil.

My advice to you is to covet the **anointing of discerning of spirits** because the ability to discern people, places and things changes the way you view them. It removes ignorance and the devil's deceptions. The following books will help you to learn about spiritual discernment and covenants:

1. **How to Discern and Expel Evil Spirits**
2. **A Teacher's Manual on Discerning and Expelling Evil Spirits**
3. **Understanding the Power of Covenants**

Chapter 18
Knowing Jesus as God by His Functions

The Lord Jesus is **a legitimate part of the Godhead** as stated in **Colossians 2:9-12:**

> "<u>**For in him dwelleth all the fullness of the Godhead bodily.**</u> *10* And ye are complete in him, which is the head of all principality and power: *11* In whom also ye are circumcised with the circumcision made without hands, in putting off the body of the sins of the flesh by the circumcision of Christ: *12* Buried with him in baptism, wherein also ye are risen with him through the faith of the operation of God, who hath raised him from the dead."

As a result, He functioned as the Son of God; meaning that God was in Him when He was here on earth and everything that He did pointed to that fact. We therefore need to see how He showed us that He is God by the various ways that He functioned when He was physically here.

Jesus Functioned as Elohim

The Lord Jesus is the 2nd person in the **Godhead** or **Elohim** and as a result, is God. As I discussed in the book, *Experiencing the Depths of God the Father (page 103):*

> *"**Elohim** is the plural of **Eloah;** it is the <u>plural form</u> of God that we refer to as the Godhead (God the Father, God the Son and God the Holy Ghost). This is where the belief in the Trinity or the Triune God began because **they are three persons in one God and we refer to them as the Godhead.** This is why when God was talking in **Genesis 1:26** He said:*

*'Let **Us** make man in **our** own image and after **our** likeness...'"*

Elohim is the name and title under which the Godhead creates. Therefore, the Lord Jesus came to help us see how **Elohim** works; meaning that He came to show us how God creates. To see the Lord Jesus functioning as **Elohim**, you need to look at **John 9:1-7**, because it reveals what happened when He encountered a man that was born without eyes. As **Elohim**, the Lord Jesus picked up clay from the ground, spat on the clay and made eyes for him thus:

> "**And as Jesus passed by, he saw a man which was blind from his birth.** 2 And his disciples asked him, saying, Master, who did sin, this man, or his parents, that he was born blind? 3 Jesus answered, Neither hath this man sinned, nor his parents: **but that the works of God should be made manifest in him.** 4 I must work the works of him that sent me, while it is day: the night cometh, when no man can work.
>
> 5 As long as I am in the world, I am the light of the world. 6 **When he had thus spoken, he spat on the ground, and made clay of the spittle, and he anointed the eyes of the blind man with the clay,** 7 And said unto him, Go, wash in the pool of Siloam, (which is by interpretation, **sent**). He went his way therefore, and washed, and came seeing."

With this miracle, we see the Lord Jesus as **Elohim;** the only God who created man, man's body parts and the rest of creation. Again, the Lord Jesus as the 2nd person that makes up **Elohim**, took the dirt of the earth; spat into it, molded it, placed it in the blind man's face for eyes and told him go wash. When the blind man washed off the clay, he had a brand new pair of eyes! In this single act, the Lord Jesus demonstrated for us how **Elohim** creates.

Therefore, if you want to know how God created Adam, all you have to do is really take a good look at this particular miracle that was done by the Lord Jesus and you will see for yourself how Adam was created. It is amazing to see that God created you and me exactly this way in Adam!

Jesus Functioned as the Almighty and the All-Sufficient One

Another way that the Lord Jesus demonstrated Himself for us as the **God** who is **Almighty** and **All-Sufficient** is in **Mark 8:1-9**. No sane, rational, or normal human being will take thousands of people into the wilderness for days and not make serious arrangements for how to feed them along the way but the Lord did because He was their sufficiency. The Lord never worried about what or how to feed those who went into the wilderness with Him:

> "In those days the multitude being very great, and having nothing to eat, Jesus called his disciples unto him, and saith unto them, 2 **I have compassion on the multitude, because they have now been with me three days, and have nothing to eat: 3 And if I send them away fasting to their own houses, they will faint by the way: for divers of them came from far.**
>
> 4 And his disciples answered him, From whence can a man satisfy these men with bread here in the wilderness? 5 **And he asked them, How many loaves have ye? And they said, Seven. 6 And he commanded the people to sit down on the ground: and he took the seven loaves, and gave thanks, and brake, and gave to his**

disciples to set before them; and they did set them before the people.

7 **And they had a few small fishes: and he blessed, and commanded to set them also before them. *8* So they did eat, and were filled**: and they took up of the broken meat that was left **seven baskets**. *9* **And they that had eaten were about four thousand:** and he sent them away."

In the days of the Lord Jesus, when you want to see God as the **Almighty** and the **All-Sufficient One**, all you had to do is take a look at the Lord Jesus. From the seven loaves of bread and few fishes, He fed the multitude of about four thousand people! After they all ate, they picked up seven baskets full of 'leftovers'. This is one of the ways that the Lord Jesus showed us both the mindset and the ways of God as the **Almighty** and the **All-Sufficient One**; He provides.

Jesus Functioned as the I AM

The Lord Jesus introduced Himself to the Jews in His days in **John 8:55-59** as the **I AM**, but they would not receive Him as such. It was sad because He was right there to provide all that they could ever need but they would not accept Him and as a result, many of them missed out on what God had for them:

"Yet ye have not known him; but I know him: and if I should say, I know him not, I shall be a liar like unto you: but I know him, and keep his saying. *56* **Your father Abraham rejoiced to see my day: and he saw it, and was glad.**

57 Then said the Jews unto him, Thou art not yet fifty years old, and hast thou seen Abraham? *58* **Jesus said unto them, Verily, verily, I say**

unto you, Before Abraham was, I am. *59* Then took they up stones to cast at him: but Jesus hid himself, and went out of the temple, going through the midst of them, and so passed by."

We saw in a previous chapter how that the Lord Jesus is the **I AM.** What we need to know now is that He can show up and deliver you or do whatever you need Him to, at any given time. You might be in need of healing, you might be in need of spiritual deliverance from demonic oppression, or you might be in need of restoration of a relationship and His promise to you is, "**I AM** more than able to do all of them and more." It is sad that the Jewish leaders failed to see Him as the **I AM**. His question to you in **Jeremiah 32:27** is:

"Behold, **I am** the LORD, the God of all flesh: **is there anything too hard for me?**"

As the **I AM**, the Lord Jesus raised up Lazarus from the dead even after Lazarus had been dead 4 days! It is never too late for the **I AM** when you call on Him in the name of the LORD JESUS. Learn from the mistakes of the Jewish leaders of Jesus' days and do not miss out on what He has for you. His desire is to help you succeed in life and to give you eternal life.

On the other hand, there were those who believed and were able to receive what they needed from Him. For instance, there was a day that the Lord Jesus was in someone's house and some men decided to bring their friend suffering from a sickness called **palsy** *(paralysis)* to the Lord so that He could heal him. They could not get to the Lord or into the house because there were so many people in the house. Therefore, they tore up the roof of the house and lowered the sick man down before the Lord Jesus.

The Bible says that when the Lord saw the faith of the sick man's friends, He was very moved by it and He said to the man that was sick, "Your sins are forgiven you." But the scribes and Pharisees that were present began to murmur saying that Jesus was speaking blasphemy **because only God** *(the I AM)* **can forgive sin.** The Lord Jesus in order to prove to them that He was indeed, the **I AM**, turned to the man sick with the *palsy* and said, "take up your bed and walk."

Below is an account of the event in **Mark 2:1-12**. You can see how **the Lord Jesus operated as the I AM in <u>forgiving sins</u> and <u>demonstrating His healing powers</u>:**

> "And again he entered into Capernaum after some days; and it was noised that he was in the house. 2 And straightway many were gathered together, insomuch that there was no room to receive them, no, not so much as about the door: and he preached the word unto them. 3 And they come unto him, bringing one sick of the palsy, which was borne of four.
>
> 4 And when they could not come nigh unto him for the press, they uncovered the roof where he was: and when they had broken it up, they let down the bed wherein the sick of the palsy lay. 5 **When Jesus saw their faith, he said unto the sick of the palsy, Son, thy sins be forgiven thee.** 6 But there were certain of the scribes sitting there, and reasoning in their hearts,
>
> 7 <u>Why doth this man thus speak blasphemies?</u> **<u>who can forgive sins but God only?</u>** 8 And immediately when Jesus perceived in his spirit that they so reasoned within themselves, he said unto them, Why reason ye these things in your hearts? 9 Whether is it easier to say to the sick of the palsy, Thy sins be forgiven thee; or to say, Arise, and take up thy bed, and walk? 10

But that ye may know that the Son of man hath power on earth to forgive sins, (he saith to the sick of the palsy,)

11 I say unto thee, Arise, and take up thy bed, and go thy way into thine house. 12 And immediately he arose, took up the bed, and went forth before them all; insomuch that they were all amazed, and glorified God, saying, We never saw it on this fashion."

During His earthly ministry days, the Lord Jesus as the **I AM** rebuked sicknesses and diseases, healed the sick, and cast out devils. Whatever they needed Him to be and do, He was there to do it as the **I AM THAT I AM**. Meaning that He was there for the Jews then and **He is now here to deliverer you, to heal you and to provide for you whatever you need at any time.** Because the Lord Jesus came to the earth to show us the **I AM THAT I AM, it** is written in the **Acts 10:38** as follows:

"**How God anointed Jesus of Nazareth with the Holy Ghost and with power: who went about doing good, and healing all that were oppressed of the devil; for God was with him**."

In the scripture above, you see that the Lord Jesus is the **I AM** in action; ever ready for whatever you and I need or ask.

Jesus Functioned as Our Victory Over Adverse Situations

The Lord Jesus is our Banner of Victory or **Jehovah Nissi**. He demonstrated **Jehovah Nissi** to us when the disciples were at sea and the sea was raging and they became afraid of their boat capsizing. **As a result, they began to scream and in response, the Lord Jesus just walked over on the sea to save them!**

Peter saw Him and said, Lord if it is you, just tell me to come to you and He said to Peter, "come." Peter got out of the boat and immediately began to walk on water; riding on the Lord's Word, **"come."** To cut the story short, He rebuked the raging sea and saved His disciples as recorded in **Matthew 14:23-33:**

> "And when he had sent the multitudes away, he went up into a mountain apart to pray: and when the evening was come, he was there alone. 24 But the ship was now in the midst of the sea, tossed with waves: for the wind was contrary. 25 **And in the fourth watch of the night Jesus went unto them, walking on the sea**.
>
> 26 And when the disciples saw him walking on the sea, they were troubled, saying, It is a spirit; and they cried out for fear. 27 **But straightway Jesus spake unto them, saying, Be of good cheer; it is I; be not afraid.** 28 **And Peter answered him and said, Lord, if it be thou, bid me come unto thee on the water.**
>
> 29 **And he said, Come, And when Peter was come down out of the ship, he walked on the water, to go to Jesus.** 30 But when he saw the wind boisterous, he was afraid; and beginning to sink, he cried, saying, Lord, save me. 31 **And immediately Jesus stretched forth his hand, and caught him, and said unto him, O thou of little faith, wherefore didst thou doubt?**
>
> 32 And when they were come into the ship, the wind ceased. 33 Then they that were in the ship came and worshipped him, saying, **Of a truth thou art the Son of God.**"

As our VICTORY, the Lord Jesus moved in the supernatural everyday of His adult life from the day of His baptism.

Jesus Functioned as the Light of the World

The Lord informed us that He is the light of the world in **John 8:12:**

> "Then spake Jesus again unto them, saying, **I am the light of the world: he that followeth me shall not walk in darkness, but shall have the light of life.**"

And again in **John 9:5:**

> "As long as I am in the world, **I am the light of the world.**"

When you truly follow Him by living according to His Word (the Word of God), you will never fail or be lost as He is the very Word of God Himself. God's Word cannot fail and it does not return to God void or with its mission unfulfilled. Therefore, the Word of God is the only light that there is in this dark world and it takes the Holy Spirit to help us understand it:

> "<u>Thy Word</u> is <u>a lamp unto my feet</u> and a <u>light unto my path</u>" (Psalm 119:105).

Jesus Functioned as the Judge of Pontius Pilate

While He was on trial before Pontius Pilate, He was very aware of the vast extent of His own powers and the limited power that both the Jews and Pontius Pilate had over Him. Actually, Pontius Pilate was pompous about the power that he thought he had over the Lord Jesus. He told the Lord that he had power to set him free or to crucify Him. In response, the Lord Jesus looked at him and promptly told him that if God had not given him power over Him, he would be powerless over Him. —**John 19:11:**

> "Jesus answered, <u>Thou couldest have no power at all against me, except it were given thee from above</u>: **therefore he that delivered me unto thee hath the greater sin.**"

One of the interesting things about the Lord Jesus is that when He was on earth, He was very aware of why He was on earth. He was very focus on pleasing His Father and so, He chose to live a sinless life. What this means is that He perfectly obeyed God as we discussed in a previous chapter. Therefore, His Father turned the judgment against all who rebel against God over to Him. **As a result, we see that the Lord judged His accusers right there at His own trial.**

He judged Pontius Pilate with a lesser sin than those of the Jewish leaders that delivered Him to Pontius Pilate. He said that the Jewish leaders had the greater sin because the Bible says that it was out of envy that they delivered up the Lord to be crucified. Even Pontius Pilot knew that it was because of envy that they delivered Him up because he could see that the Jewish leaders were jealous of the Lord Jesus.

They also confessed to themselves that if they left Him alone, the Romans would come and take away their precious positions, so, according to them, it was better for Him to die than for them to lose their positions of privilege. They were not seeking true judgment; all they wanted was to get rid of the Lord Jesus as shown in **John 11:47:50:**

> "Then gathered the chief priests and the Pharisees a council, and said, What do we? for this man doeth many miracles. 48 **If we let him thus alone, all men will believe on him: and the Romans shall come and take away both our**

place and nation. 49 And one of them, named Caiaphas, being the high priest that same year, said unto them, Ye know nothing at all, 50 Nor consider that it is expedient for us, that one man should die for the people, and that the whole nation perish not."

Simply put, the Lord Jesus was bad for their selfish ways, so they wanted Him out of the way by crying loudly for Him to be crucified and for this, the Lord judged them.

Jesus Functioned as the Judge of the Devil

Again, God the Father has committed all Judgments to the Son, so when the devil came against Him, the devil lost his **Adam-given authority** to rule and judge on earth. Before the coming of the Lord Jesus, **the devil had been using his corrupt legal and religious systems to enslave and kill human beings and he had been getting away with it because "all had sinned" but when he came against the Lord Jesus, he came against one who had not sinned.**

The Lord was sinless: even after His examination by scourging, both King Herod and Pontius Pilate declared that they "find no fault in Him;" yet, the devil used his corrupt systems of the Jewish leaders and Pontius Pilate to <u>execute Him</u> rather than <u>acquit Him</u>. As a result, the devil lost his Adam-given authority on earth and the Lord already foresaw this hence He said in **John 16:11:**

"The prince of this world is judged."

According to the natural laws that God gave man on earth, when a person is found innocent of a crime, the person is to be set free or acquitted. The devil in his eagerness to get rid of the Lord Jesus from the earth; transgressed this law and was found guilty of being an <u>unjust Judge</u>. God is man's last Court of Appeal so, He acquitted the Lord Jesus

175

and brought Him back to life because He was unjustly condemned. **He then judged the devil for his miscarriage of justice. Thus, the prince of this world was forever judged.** Consequently, the Lord was able to legally take back the authority over the earth that Adam had given to the devil.

Conclusion

Worshipping the Lord Jesus Christ is not the worshipping of a mere man or one that is not truly God as some in other religions want people to believe or as the atheists claim in their attempts to challenge or to debate the existence of God or the identity of Jesus Christ. In this book, I showed you from scriptures how that the Lord Jesus is who He said He was — the Son of God!

Take Him at His Word so that you can walk with Him because when you walk with Him, you will not walk in darkness. By submitting to His Lordship, you make yourself available to receive eternal life and for Him to further reveal Himself to you. Therefore, you must be willing to exercise faith in God's Word because failure to do this means rebellion in the sight of God and you will not get anything out of Him when you choose to walk in unbelief towards Him and His Word.

If you already know Him and He is your Lord, you are on the right track but if not, I advise you to call on the name of the Lord Jesus today because He is waiting for you to do so. He extended His invitation to you in **Revelation 3:20** below, so make sure that you respond to Him today:

> **"Behold, I stand at the door** *(your heart)*, **and knock: <u>if any man hear my voice, and open the door</u>, I will come in to him, and will sup with him, and he with me."**

This book is His voice speaking to you and inviting you to open the door of your heart to Him. I hope you will respond. Below is How to Respond to Him in **Romans 10:9-11:**

> **"That if thou shalt confess with thy mouth the Lord Jesus, and shalt believe in thine**

heart that God hath raised him from the dead, thou shalt be saved. *10* For with the heart man believeth unto righteousness; and with the mouth confession is made unto salvation. *11* For the scripture saith, Whosoever believeth on him shall not be ashamed."

Below is a prayer that will help you confess your faith in the Lord Jesus Christ. Be sure to pray the prayer out loud so that your declaration of faith can be heard in the spiritual realm by God the Father. Also, the devil can hear you reject him.

Confession of Faith in the Lord Jesus Christ:

"Lord Jesus, I believe with all my heart and I confess with my mouth that You are the Son of God and that You came into this world as God's lamb. You died on the Cross for my sin and You were buried and on the 3rd day, God the Father raised You up again from the dead. Lord Jesus, come into my heart and be my Lord. I repent of all my sins and I ask You to forgive me and wash them away with Your blood.

I turn my life over to You to lead and guide me with Your Word. Also, I ask that You baptize me with the Holy Spirit to keep me, teach me the Bible and help me live my life for You. Lord Jesus, I choose to forsake all other religions and follow You as the only true way to God (John 14:6). Amen."

May the Lord bless you abundantly.

— Dr. Mary J. Ogenaarekhua

About the Author

I am a born again Christian who believes in the preservation of human life and the sanctity of marriage as defined by the Bible. Below is the biographical information about me.

Biographical Information

Name: Prophetess Mary J. Ogenaarekhua, PhD (pronounced **Oge-nah-re-qua**).

Founder: Mary J. Ministries, Inc.

Educational Background: BA Communications-Journalism, Masters Degree in Public Administration and a PhD in Theology

Dr. Mary Justina Ogenaarekhua (a.k.a Mary O.) was born in Nigeria. She grew up in a Muslim home and attended Roman Catholic elementary and high schools. The Lord miraculously raised Mary up from the dead when she took a fatal fall in her early years. Prophetess Mary has an eagle's eye that sees far into the realm of the spirit and is gifted with the ability to interpret visions and dreams, to hear the voice of the Lord, to discern spirits and to intercede as a prayer warrior. She is also the Lord's scribe.

Dr. Mary operates in the gift of prophecy and God has opened Prophetess Mary's spiritual eyes to see His desire for His people. She is a teacher of the unadulterated Word of God; a true woman of God in rare spiritual form! She holds workshops and conferences as well as teaches and preaches on many topics including **deliverance, healing,** visions and dreams, spiritual discernment, understanding the power of covenants, effective prayer, mentoring, leadership training and much more. She conducts **evangelism and outdoor crusades internationally** with thousands in attendance.

Dr. Mary Justina Ogenaarekhua is the author of the following books:

(1) **Unveiling the God-Mother.** This book is a biography of *Mary's death and resurrection experience* and her early years in Africa. It details the spiritual events that happened to her before she became a Christian and before she came to the United States. She also discusses some of the holidays that a lot of Christians celebrate ignorantly.

(2) **Keys to Understanding Your Visions and Dreams: A Classroom Approach.** In this book about visions and dreams, she uses the Word of God to instruct the body of Christ on visions and dreams. She applies the first hand revelation knowledge that she learned from the Lord Himself. This book is a must read for everyone who dreams and everyone who sees visions. It will teach you how to interpret them with the Word of God.

(3) **A Teacher's Manual on Visions and Dreams.** This manual is designed to teach the average person, bishops, pastors, etc., the basic principles about visions and dreams, about sources of vision and dreams, about how to identify the sources of visions and dreams and how to analyze the contents of visions and dreams. It is meant to be used along with the above textbook titled, **Keys to Understanding Your Visions and Dreams.**

(4) How to Discern and Expel Evil Spirits. This is a very powerful book for all those who are called to the healing and deliverance ministry. In it, Dr. Mary answers the questions most people have concerning evil spirits, and she teaches on the origin of evil spirits, how to discern and expel them and she answers the question, "Can a Christian have a demon?" This is a foundational resource for all those who want to walk in great spiritual discernment.

(5) A Teacher's Manual on Discerning and Expelling Evil Spirits. This is a powerful teaching guide for those who are called to the healing and deliverance ministry. It is a teacher's tool with a step by step teaching on key principles about evil spirits, the origin of evil spirits and how to identify and expel evil spirits. It is meant to be used along with the above textbook on **How to Discern and Expel Evil Spirits**.

(6) How I Heard from God: The Power of Personal Prophesy. Prophetess Mary Ogenaarekhua outlines key principles concerning personal prophecy and she lays out a blue print of what to do with your personal prophetic words. She helps the reader understand the conditions that are attached by God to every personal prophetic word. Failure to understand these conditions will keep your God-given prophetic word from coming to pass.

(7) Effective Prayers for Various Situations: Volumes I and II. In *Effective Prayers*, Prophetess Mary outlines principles on how to pray effectively concerning various life situations. It contains prayers for almost every situation that a lot of Christians battle with. Many have given testimonies about the deliverance and blessings manifested in their lives as a result of praying these prayers.

(8) Keys to Successful Mentoring Relationships. In this book, Dr. Mary outlines the dynamics involved in a mentoring relationship and the actual steps and stages of mentoring. She also highlights the pitfalls to avoid.

(9) A Workbook for Successful Mentoring. This workbook is a powerful teaching guide for all those who want to be mentored and those who desire to mentor others. It is a teacher/student's valuable tool for teaching and practicing mentoring. It is meant to be used along with the above textbook titled, **Keys to Successful Mentoring Relationships**.

(10) Understanding the Power of Covenants. This book teaches on the power of covenants. Covenants impact our lives for good or for bad on a daily basis. It allows us to learn about how God uses covenants, how the devil uses covenants and how God wants us to use covenants so that we can receive what He has for us and avoid the devil's attempts to use negative covenants to hinder us. Negative covenants can hinder a person's progress throughout the person's life.

(11) Secrets About Writing and Publishing Your Book: What Other Publishers Will Not Tell You. This book is a powerful synopsis of what you need to know in order to write and get your book published and also how to position your book for mass marketing. It is designed to help all those who desire to write and market their books.

(12) The Agenda of the Few. This book is a call for the Church to get back to its God-given purpose for this country which is to reach all Americans for God. For too long now, the Church has been functioning as though it is only called to one political party –the Republican Party. The issues discussed in this book are meant to remind the reader that there are Ten Commandments in the Bible and that God can choose to address any of these commandments at any given time. Therefore, we must be willing to get the Church out of the Republican Party box that we have placed it in and learn to seek God's will during each presidential election. He is God of both the Republican and Democratic Parties.

(13) **The Agenda of the Masses.** Just like the **"Agenda of the Few"** that was written to the Christian Conservatives in the Republican Party, this book addresses what the Lord showed me that a lot of the Christians in the Democratic Party are doing that equally displeases Him. They have allowed a very large segment of the Church to be pulled away by "the agenda of the masses." In other words, they have bought into the ungodly doctrines, ideologies, beliefs, and political views of the masses to the point that now, their version of Christianity within the Democratic Party is essentially "anything goes." In their attempt to please the masses, they have embraced the pagan gods and have lumped their worship together with the worship of the Judeo-Christian God of the Bible.

(14) **What Tribe of Israel Am I From?** This book is designed to answer the questions of some Christians who are trying to determine the tribe of the natural Israel that they are from. The reason they want to know this is because there are some teachings going on in Christendom in which Christians are being assigned to the various tribes of Israel. This book will help anyone to determine the tribe of Israel that they are from. It is an eye opener for anyone who desires to know the truth.

(15) **Experiencing the Depths of God the Father.** This book is the first in a series of three books titled, *Experiencing*

the Depths of God the Father, Experiencing the Depths of Jesus Christ, and *Experiencing the Depths of the Holy Spirit.* It is written to help you know God in depth as well as understand the mysteries that He has coded in His Word for you. Therefore, this book is for you if you want to know God in a deeper way so that you can receive all that He has for you. It is truly a book for all those who want to know God in a deeper more intimate way.

Dr. Mary O. lives in Atlanta and is the founder of **Mary J. Ministries** and **To His Glory Publishing Company, Inc.** She is an ordained minister with a strong Deliverance Anointing. She has appeared on Trinity Broadcasting Network and other national television programs.

About Mary J. Ministries

Mary J. Ministries was founded by Dr. Mary J. Ogenaarekhua to equip and impart the Anointing of God to the Body of Christ for the purpose of impacting the whole world. Our mission is to help men, women; old and the young to build relationships through Bible Studies, Community Outreach, Prayer Support, Caring Ministries, Teaching on Visions and Dreams, Discernment/Deliverance, Evangelism, Mentoring, Fellowship and Special Events.

As an ordained minister, Prophetess Mary O. teaches, trains and activates individuals to properly operate their prophetic gifts of discernment, deliverance ministry, out-reach ministry (evangelism) and interpretation of visions and dreams. Teachings provided by Prophetess Mary O. are inspired by God and are balanced biblical principles for the purpose of developing a spirit of excellence, wholeness and GODLY character.

Prophetess Mary O. is committed to helping the Body of Christ and those who do not yet know the Lord Jesus as their personal Savior to understand their God-given purpose. Mary J. Ministries regularly hosts classes, seminars, conferences and crusades in the US, Canada as well as other countries.

Contact Mary J. Ministries:
Phone: **770-458-7947**
Website: www.maryjministries.org

About To His Glory Publishing Co.

To His Glory Publishing Company, Inc. was also founded by Dr. Mary J. Ogenaarekhua to help writers become published authors. Our goal is to help new and established writers edit, publish and market their work for a reasonable cost.

To His Glory Publishing Company, Inc. offers one of the most cost efficient and stress-free ways of getting a manuscript published.

> **We also pay one of the highest royalties in the publishing industry 40%!**

Our Services Include:
- Editing
- Book layout
- Book cover design
- Book manufacturing
- Book distribution (this is a separate and optional service)
- Book placement on Amazon.com, Barnesandnoble.com, Kindle, iPad, and other book marketing sites and devices (this is a separate and optional service).

Contact To His Glory Publishing Company:
Phone: **770-458-7947**
Website: www.tohisglorypublishing.com

Bibliography

Josephus, Flavius. *Jewish Antiquities,* Book 14, chapter 13:1 (326).

Ogenaarekhua, Mary J. *Experiencing the depths of God the Father: A Deeper Understanding of the Godhead (pages 103, 105-106).* To His Glory Publishing Company, Inc., Lilburn, USA.

Ogenaarekhua, Mary J. *What Tribe of Israel Am I From?* To His Glory Publishing Company, Inc., Lilburn, USA.

Ogenaarekhua, Mary J. *Unveiling the God mother.* To His Glory Publishing Company, Inc., Lilburn, USA.

TO HIS GLORY PUBLISHING COMPANY, INC.

463 Dogwood Dr. Lilburn, GA. 30047, U.S.A (770)458-7947

Order Form for Bookstores in the USA

Order Date: _____

Order Placed By: _____   By Fax. _____

Address: _____

_____

City _____ ST/ZIP _____

Phone #: _____

Email: _____

Purchase Order#: _____

Return Policy: Within 1 year but not before 90 Days.

Price	Quantity	List Price
Shipping Method:		
Media:		
UPS:		
FedEx:		
Other (Please Secify):		
Total Price:	**Total Quantity:**	**List Price**

Ship To Address: Bill to Address:

To His Glory Publishing

Let Us Publish Your Book

To His Glory Publishing Company will publish your book at the least expensive cost. We pay one of the highest royalties in the industry – 40%! We print on demand and place your book on the major online bookstores such a Amazon.com, Barnesandnoble.com, Bookamillion.com, etc.

Other Books by Prophetess Mary Ogenaarekhua

Understanding the Power of
COVENANTS

Dr. Mary J. Ogenaarekhua

ISBN 978-0-9791566-8-7

ISBN 978-0-9821900-2-9

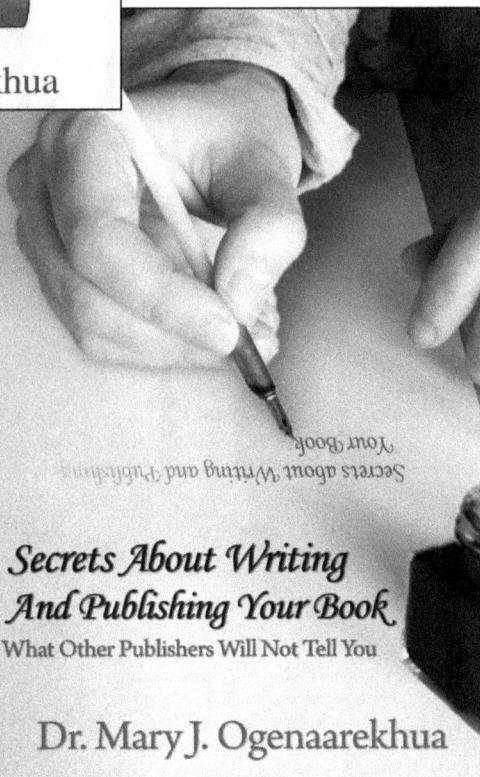

Secrets About Writing and Publishing Your Book

**Secrets About Writing
And Publishing Your Book**
What Other Publishers Will Not Tell You

Dr. Mary J. Ogenaarekhua

Other Books by Prophetess Mary Ogenaarekhua

ISBN 978-0-9774265-6-0

ISBN 978-0-9774265-9-1

EFFECTIVE PRAYERS
FOR VARIOUS SITUATIONS

Prophetess
Mary J. Ogenaarekhua
AUTHOR OF UNVEILING THE GOD-MOTHER
Vol. 1

TIVE PRAYERS
IOUS SITUATIONS
Vol. II

Prophetess
Mary J. Ogenaarekhua
AUTHOR OF UNVEILING THE GOD-MOTHER

Other Books by Prophetess Mary Ogenaarekhua

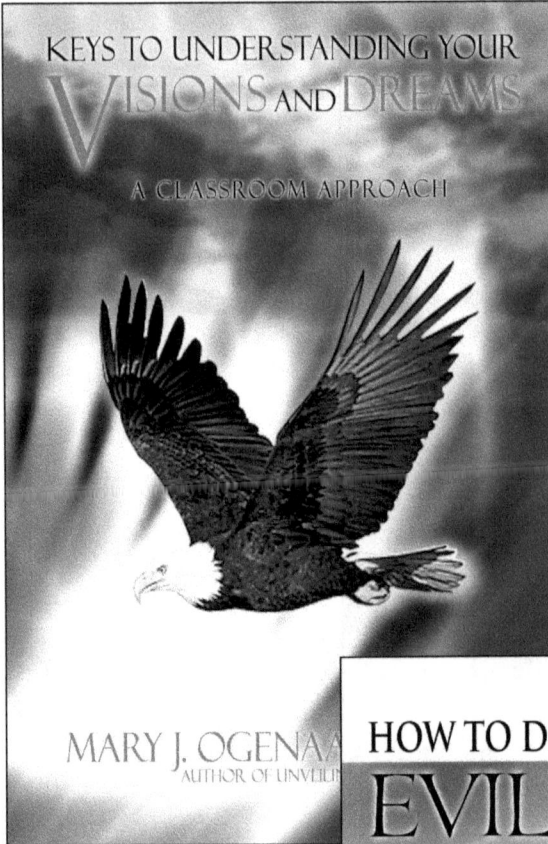

KEYS TO UNDERSTANDING YOUR
VISIONS AND DREAMS

A CLASSROOM APPROACH

MARY J. OGENAA
AUTHOR OF UNVEIL

ISBN 978-0-9749802-1-8

ISBN 978-0-9749802-8-7

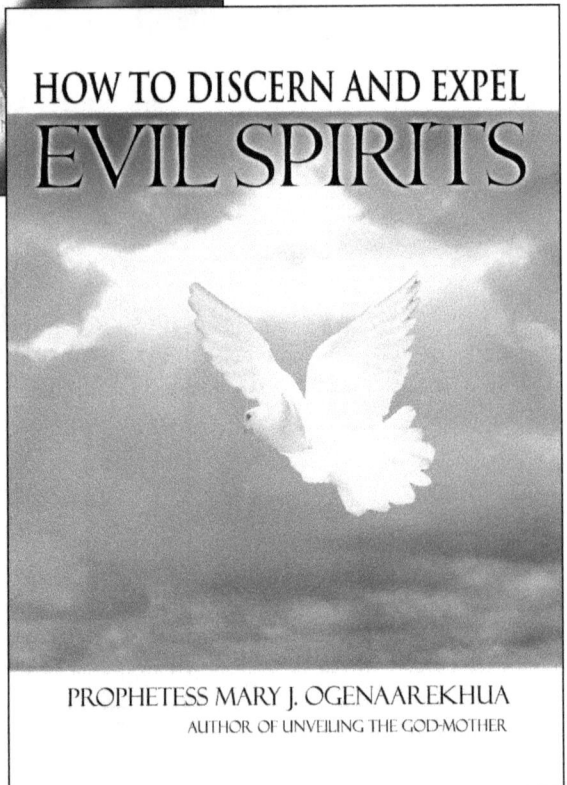

HOW TO DISCERN AND EXPEL
EVIL SPIRITS

PROPHETESS MARY J. OGENAAREKHUA
AUTHOR OF UNVEILING THE GOD-MOTHER

Other Books by Prophetess Mary Ogenaarekhua

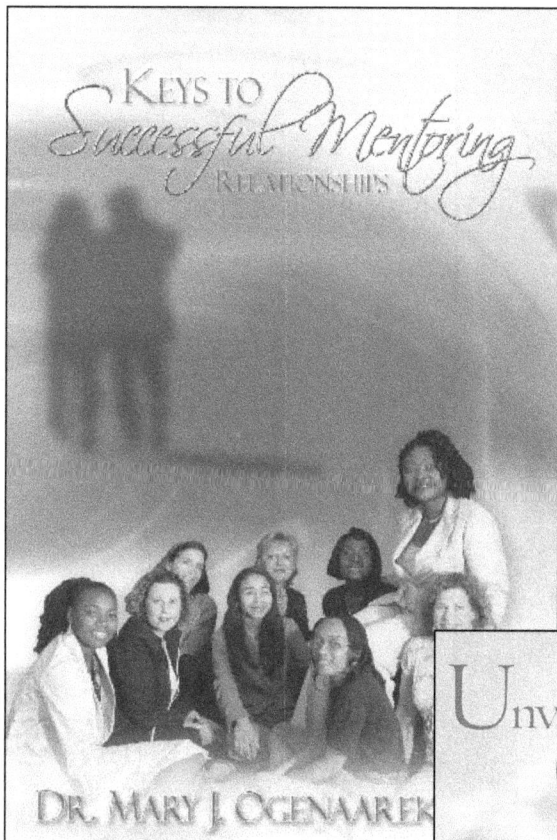

KEYS TO
Successful Mentoring
RELATIONSHIPS

DR. MARY J. OGENAAREK

ISBN 978-0-9791566-6-3

Unveiling the
God-Mother

"A real life account of one whom God raised from the dead."

Mary J. Ogenaarekhua

ISBN 978-1-5873628-0-4

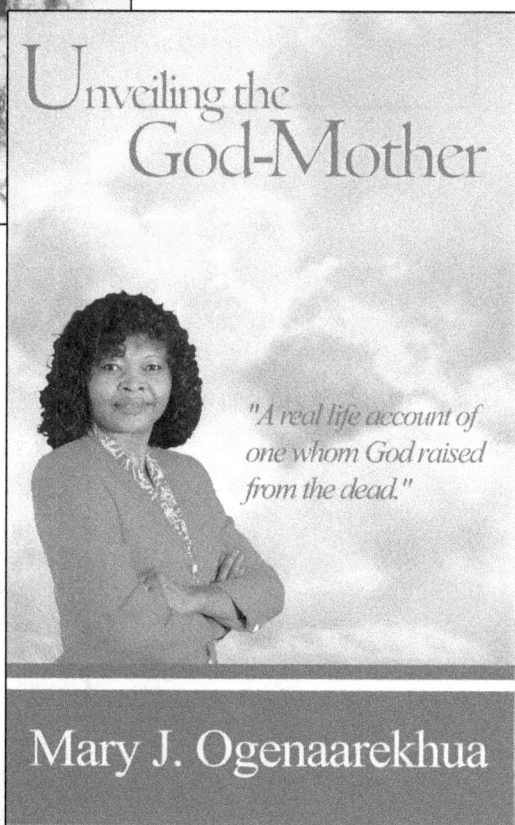

Other Books by Prophetess Mary Ogenaarekhua

ISBN 978-0-9821900-1-2

ISBN 978-0-9821900-4-3

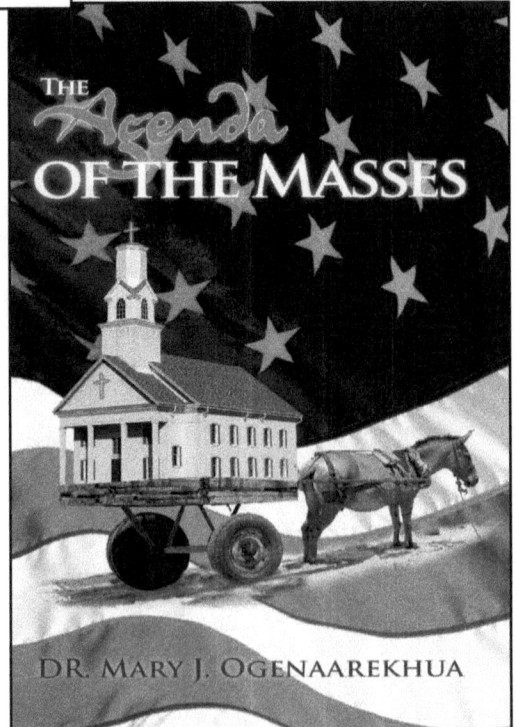

Other Books by Prophetess Mary Ogenaarekhua

ISBN 978-1-5873628-0-4

What Tribe of Israel Am I From?

Dr. Mary J. Ogenaarekhua

Experiencing The Depths of God The Father
A DEEPER UNDERSTANDING OF THE GODHEAD

DR. MARY J. OGENAAREKHUA

ISBN 978-0-9821900 -7- 4